PHP Application Development with NetBeans Beginner's Guide

Boost your PHP development skills with this step-by-step practical guide

M A Hossain Tonu

BIRMINGHAM - MUMBAI

PHP Application Development with NetBeans
Beginner's Guide

First published: August 2012

Production Reference: 1210812

Published by Packt Publishing Ltd.
Livery Place
35 Livery Street
Birmingham B3 2PB, UK.

ISBN 978-1-84951-580-1

www.packtpub.com

Cover Image by Karl Moore (karl.moore@ukonline.co.uk)

Credits

Author

M A Hossain Tonu

Reviewers

Tomáš Myšík

Deepak Hindurao Patil

Azizur Rahman

Anthony Reid

Kaiser Ahmed

Mushfiq-E Mahabub

Acquisition Editor

Kartikey Pandey

Lead Technical Editor

Dayan Hyames

Technical Editor

Lubna Shaikh

Copy Editor

Insiya Morbiwala

Project Coordinator

Sai Gamare

Proofreader

Bernadette Watkins

Indexer

Hemangini Bari

Production Coordinator

Arvindkumar Gupta

Cover Work

Arvindkumar Gupta

About the Author

M A Hossain Tonu graduated in Computer Science and Engineering from Dhaka University of Engineering and Technology (DUET) in Bangladesh. He has been a passionate developer over the past six years, has worked for leading software companies in the country, such as Somewherein and Improsys, and has developed a series of web applications, services, and solutions for foreign clients as part of the offshore software development and outsourcing team. He is an agile software craftsman, who loves to code, keep himself updated with cutting-edge technologies, and play with PHP, Zend Framework, Ruby-on-Rails, JavaScript, and more. He loves to moderate the local PHP community—phpXperts—and conducts seminars and workshops at different tech premises.

You can reach Tonu at `mahtonu@gmail.com`, and his tech blog is available at `http://mahtonu.wordpress.com`.

It takes many people to create a book like this, and I'd like to thank some people for their contributions to this work.

First of all, I would like to thank my wife Shamima Rahman Jhumur for her tremendous patience when I was unavailable to her. I appreciate my family, friends, and well-wishers, who continuously tolerate my computer madness.

To the people at Packt, I am much obliged: Kartikey Pandey, the man who started the process; Dayan Hyames, for guiding me throughout; Alka Nayak, the kind soul accepting my delays; and Lubna Shaikh, for being such a great help.

I'd also like to thank those who provided prepublication feedback, such as Ondřej Nešpor, Tomáš Myšík and Nurul Ferdous.

Lastly, I would like to dedicate this book to Hasin Hayder, the PHP mentor.

About the Reviewers

Tomáš Myšík is a Java Software Developer working on NetBeans, on its PHP support. He used to be a Java Enterprise, and PHP developer working on modern websites. In his leisure time, he likes sports (especially football and ice-hockey), reading books, and of course, learning all new things related to software development.

Deepak Patil is a Software Architect, Mobile Web Enthusiast, and Instructor of Standards-Based Mobile Web Development.

His initial responsibilities included the architecture, design, development, implementation, and support of web applications, especially into the LAMP stack.

He has eight years of experience in the Internet industry, and specializes in LAMP technologies and open source. He has experience in all areas of application development processes, including database design, user interface, e-commerce, security, web services, optimization, and scalability.

He is the Tech Lead at @netCore Solutions; is an Open Source Entrepreneur, and loves all things social, mobile, cricket, and soccer; and is a proud Indian.

Deepak holds a Masters degree in Computer Applications (2004) from Shivaji University, Kolhapur in Maharashtra, India.

Azizur Rahman is a B.Sc. (Hons) graduate in Artificial Intelligence from the University of Westminster, UK. He was first introduced to NetBeans IDE during his placement at a London-based Internet Service Provider. In his placement role, he realized the power of NetBeans IDE to develop Real Estate Management Software, which is used by the top estate agencies in London.

After graduating, Azizur secured employment with the University of Manchester as a Web Application Developer. Throughout his six years of employment with the University, he successfully used NetBeans IDE to develop a variety of internal applications. Some of his most challenging projects have been to develop secure, reliable, scalable, and robust, client-facing web applications using PHP Zend Framework and MySQL database.

In late 2011, he decided to pursue new pastures, and currently works for a world-class, broadcasting company in the UK, developing innovative web applications used by millions of users across the globe, where NetBeans IDE still firmly remains the tool of choice.

A firm believer in philanthropy, he spends his spare time supporting philanthropic causes, using his knowledge and expertise of open source technologies, and has helped international, non-profit organizations, such as Mercy Mission World; he is currently leading the development team at ProductiveMuslim.com. He uses NetBeans IDE to develop web applications, custom WordPress themes, and plugins to support his work.

His keen interest in open source software makes him a regular attendee at the Manchester WordPress User Group and wider PHP and open source community events.

I would like to thank everyone who helped in tech reviewing this book. You know who you are; you have been absolutely amazing in supporting me when I needed it most. Thank you for all your help.

Anthony Reid is a Software Developer, who currently works within the Information Systems Department of a London insurance brokerage firm. Anthony has over 20 years of programming experience. His career started in the pre-Windows era, developing database systems in DataEase, Paradox, FoxPro, and Visual Basic.

For the last 10 years, he has focused on developing an array of PHP/SQL applications covering financial risk management, workflow, and accounting solutions.

Kaiser Ahmed is a professional Web Developer. He gained his B.Sc. degree from Khulna University of Engineering and Technology (KUET), and his M.Sc. degree in Computer Science and Engineering from United International University, Dhaka. He is also a co-founder of CyberXpress.Net Inc, based in Bangladesh.

He has a wide breadth of technical skills and Internet knowledge, and has experience across the spectrum of online development in the service of building and improving online properties for multiple clients. He enjoys creating site architecture and infrastructure, backend development using open source toolsets (PHP, MySQL, Apache, Linux, and others, such as LAMP), and frontend development with CSS and HTML/XHTML.

I want to thank my loving wife, Maria Akter, for her great support.

Mushfiq-E Mahabub is a Software Engineer, driven by passion.

He has been writing production-level code for the last three years using open source technologies, such as LAMP, Python/Django, YII, Zend, MySQL, and MongoDB.

Currently, he is working as a Platform Engineer for a new start-up.

After acquiring his BSc Engineering degree in Computer Science, he participated in the development of open source software based on Python.

He has been conducting different workshops and seminars on open source software since 2009 for university students.

He writes technical notes at `http://mushfiq.com` on a regular basis.

www.PacktPub.com

Support files, eBooks, discount offers and more

You might want to visit www.PacktPub.com for support files and downloads related to your book.

Did you know that Packt offers eBook versions of every book published, with PDF and ePub files available? You can upgrade to the eBook version at www.PacktPub.com and as a print book customer, you are entitled to a discount on the eBook copy. Get in touch with us at service@packtpub.com for more details.

At www.PacktPub.com, you can also read a collection of free technical articles, sign up for a range of free newsletters and receive exclusive discounts and offers on Packt books and eBooks.

http://PacktLib.PacktPub.com

Do you need instant solutions to your IT questions? PacktLib is Packt's online digital book library. Here, you can access, read and search across Packt's entire library of books.

Why Subscribe?

- Fully searchable across every book published by Packt
- Copy and paste, print and bookmark content
- On demand and accessible via web browser

Free Access for Packt account holders

If you have an account with Packt at www.PacktPub.com, you can use this to access PacktLib today and view nine entirely free books. Simply use your login credentials for immediate access.

Table of Contents

Preface

Productivity is an important factor for a software developer. A good development environment or surrounding tools with the essence of a particular programming flavor can boost up our coding productivity and yield a quality and optimized software product. In order to maintain a fast-paced development, developers seek the environment with which they feel at home. Such an Integrated Development Environment (IDE) can really accelerate code implementation and be the magic wand to your project development.

A good IDE is more like a Swiss army knife with crafted features. It consists of:

- A source editor
- A compiler/an interpreter
- A debugger
- Database management support
- Version Control System
- Tools for Object-Oriented Programming, such as Class Browser and Object Inspector

IDE, like NetBeans, comes with greater flexibility, with such features where the developer can feel at home. Moreover, NetBeans is absolutely free of charge and is provided by the open source community. Simply put, the IDE for PHP will facilitate your productivity from development to production, in every respect.

In this book, *PHP Application Development with NetBeans Beginner's Guide*, you will learn how to cover different categories of web-based applications with the help of NetBeans IDE through a couple of real-life, trendy PHP projects, and will complete the book as a confident PHP developer.

What this book covers

Chapter 1, Setting Up Your Development Environment, guides you through the process of NetBeans installation and sets up the PHP development environment step by step. By the end of this chapter, you will have your development environment ready on your operating system.

Chapter 2, Boosting Your Coding Productivity with PHP Editor, shows how you can write faster code using the NetBeans PHP Editor. You will be introduced to killer features of the IDE, such as code completion, code templates, rename refactoring, and code generation. At the end of this chapter, you will have a full, hands-on knowledge of the editor's smart features and increased coding productivity.

Chapter 3, Building a Facebook-like Status Poster using NetBeans, jumps directly to a real-life, PHP application development that will be used to display Facebook/Twitter-like, posted status streams. By the end of this chapter, you will be able to develop simple PHP applications with the NetBeans IDE.

Chapter 4, Debugging and Testing using NetBeans, will explain how to debug and test a PHP application using the IDE. Topics covered in the chapter include configuring XDebug, debugging the PHP source code, testing with PHPUnit and Selenium, and code coverage.

Chapter 5, Using Code Documentation, guides the developer through the process of creating source and project documentation. You will become familiar with PHPDoc standard tags and their use, to document the source code with the help of the editor. Also, you will use an external document generator for the project API.

Chapter 6, Understanding Git, the NetBeans Way, will show you how to use Git, a free and open source-distributed version control system. Using the IDE, you will be working on Git operations, such as initializing or cloning a repository, staging files, committing changes, reverting modifications, and remote repository operations such as fetching, pulling, and pushing, while working with branches. By the end of this chapter, you will be able to be part of a development team using the NetBeans collaborative development feature.

Chapter 7, Building User Registration, Login, and Logout, deals with a professional PHP application. You will design and develop a PHP application where users can register themselves, and after the registration they can log in to the application, view, and update their own profile, and more.

Appendix A, Introducing Symfony2 Support in NetBeans 7.2, will discover the Symfony2 PHP framework support by NetBeans. This introduces Symfony2's project creation, runs Symfony2 commands, and introduces bundle creation from NetBeans.

Appendix B, NetBeans Keyboard Shortcuts, is a convenient reference for common NetBeans keyboard shortcuts.

What you need for this book

In *Chapter 1, Setting up your Development Environment* the *Recommended system requirements* section, explains the system requirements, and the sections beginning with *Setting up your development environment* explains the PHP development environment for specific operating systems. In summary, you should have the following:

- ◆ NetBeans IDE
- ◆ Latest package of Apache, MySQL, and PHP

Who this book is for

The book is aimed at beginning level PHP developers who wish to develop PHP applications while taking advantage of the NetBeans functionality to ease their software development efforts and utilize the powerful features of the IDE. Familiarity with NetBeans is not assumed. However, a little familiarity with PHP development is expected.

Conventions

In this book, you will find several headings appearing frequently.

To give clear instructions on how to complete a procedure or task, we use:

Time for action – heading

1. Action 1
2. Action 2
3. Action 3

Instructions often need some extra explanation so that they make sense, so they are followed with:

What just happened?

This heading explains the working of tasks or instructions that you have just completed.

You will also find some other learning aids in the book, including:

Pop quiz – heading

These are short multiple choice questions intended to help you test your own understanding.

Have a go hero – heading

These set practical challenges and give you ideas for experimenting with what you have learned.

You will also find a number of styles of text that distinguish between different kinds of information. Here are some examples of these styles, and an explanation of their meaning.

Code words in text are shown as follows: "Set the `installation` folder using the file browser."

A block of code is set as follows:

```php
<?php
echo "Hello World";
?>
```

When we wish to draw your attention to a particular part of a code block, the relevant lines or items are set in bold:

```html
<head>
  <meta http-equiv="Content-Type" content="text/html;
    charset=UTF-8">
  <title>Status updater</title>
  <link href="<?=BASE_URL?>styles/styles.css" media="screen"
    rel="stylesheet" type="text/css" />
  <script src="http://ajax.googleapis.com/ajax/
    libs/jquery/1.7/jquery.min.js">
  </script>
  <script src="<?=BASE_URL?>js/status.js"></script>
</head>
```

Any command-line input or output is written as follows:

```
sudo apt-get install lamp-server^
```

New terms and **important words** are shown in bold. Words that you see on the screen, in menus or dialog boxes, for example, appear in the text like this: "By clicking on the **Next** button, you will be asked to accept the license agreement."

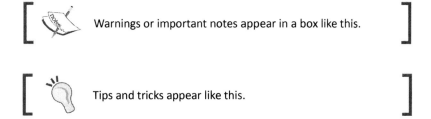

Warnings or important notes appear in a box like this.

Tips and tricks appear like this.

Reader feedback

Feedback from our readers is always welcome. Let us know what you think about this book—what you liked or may have disliked. Reader feedback is important for us to develop titles that you really get the most out of.

To send us general feedback, simply send an e-mail to feedback@packtpub.com, and mention the book title via the subject of your message.

If there is a book that you need and would like to see us publish, please send us a note in the **SUGGEST A TITLE** form on www.packtpub.com or e-mail suggest@packtpub.com.

If there is a topic that you have expertise in and you are interested in either writing or contributing to a book, see our author guide on www.packtpub.com/authors.

Customer support

Now that you are the proud owner of a Packt book, we have a number of things to help you to get the most from your purchase.

Downloading the example code

You can download the example code files for all Packt books you have purchased from your account at http://www.PacktPub.com. If you purchased this book elsewhere, you can visit http://www.PacktPub.com/support and register to have the files e-mailed directly to you.

Errata

Although we have taken every care to ensure the accuracy of our content, mistakes do happen. If you find a mistake in one of our books—maybe a mistake in the text or the code—we would be grateful if you would report this to us. By doing so, you can save other readers from frustration and help us improve subsequent versions of this book. If you find any errata, please report them by visiting http://www.packtpub.com/support, selecting your book, clicking on the **errata submission form** link, and entering the details of your errata. Once your errata are verified, your submission will be accepted and the errata will be uploaded on our website, or added to any list of existing errata, under the Errata section of that title. Any existing errata can be viewed by selecting your title from http://www.packtpub.com/support.

Piracy

Piracy of copyright material on the Internet is an ongoing problem across all media. At Packt, we take the protection of our copyright and licenses very seriously. If you come across any illegal copies of our works, in any form, on the Internet, please provide us with the location address or website name immediately so that we can pursue a remedy.

Please contact us at copyright@packtpub.com with a link to the suspected pirated material.

We appreciate your help in protecting our authors, and our ability to bring you valuable content.

Questions

You can contact us at questions@packtpub.com if you are having a problem with any aspect of the book, and we will do our best to address it.

1
Setting up your Development Environment

*NetBeans is a free and open source **Integrated Development Environment (IDE)**, which complies with multiple programming languages. For a long time it has been the editor of choice to major developer communities. Along with the growing market demand, NetBeans has integrated the PHP development features since NetBeans 6.5 (November 2008), and these days, it has become one of the most popular IDEs for the PHP community.*

In this chapter we will discuss:

- Why NetBeans for PHP application development?
- Downloading the NetBeans IDE
- Step-by-step NetBeans installation
- Setting up your PHP development environment
- Creating a NetBeans project

So let's get on with it...

Why NetBeans for PHP application development?

NetBeans IDE facilitates our daily PHP application development activities with the following:

- **Creating and managing projects**: The IDE for PHP enables us to create PHP projects, and helps to grow the project. It can perform project-related settings and operations; that is, creating documentation for the project, testing the project, and so on.

- **Editing features for the source code**: The code editor comes with an exciting collection of source-editing capabilities within the PHP project scope. It empowers faster code writing with the following features:

  - **Syntax highlighting** enables highlighting PHP syntax in project files.

  - **Code folding** enables the folding and unfolding of selected classes and method codes within the current file.

  - **Navigation** helps to explore classes and methods in the current PHP file.

  - **Code templates** help in using predefined code snippets.

  - **Code completion** shows the code's auto completion list.

  - **Parameter hints** give information about the formal parameters of a method where the method is called.

  - **Smart indent** provides auto formatting while code pressing.

  - **Formatting** provides auto code formatting in the current file.

  - **Bracket completion** adds/removes paired quotes, parentheses, and braces during code writing.

  - **Mark occurrences** marks all the occurrences of a code string within the opened project files.

  - **Error detection** shows the PHP parsing error immediately after typing is finished.

  - **Pair matching** highlights matched pair of quotes, braces, parentheses, and so on.

  - **Semantic highlighting** identifies the keywords, method names, call, unused variables, and so on.

  - **Go to declaration** sends the cursor to where the chosen type is declared.

- ❏ **Instant rename** renames all occurrences of a variable within its scope.
- ❏ **Spell checker** shows spelling mistakes and corrections.
- ❏ **Code documentation** helps with an automatic documentation structure.

- ◆ **Deploying the project**: Provides synchronization within the PHP project content, with remote server content.

- ◆ **Database and services**: Provides support for database management and web services.

- ◆ **SCM tools**: Provides source code management tools, such as Git, Subversion, CVS, and Mercurial, built-in for source code versioning, tracking changes, and so on.

- ◆ **Running PHP scripts**: Enables the parsing of PHP scripts, and yields output within the IDE without going to the browser.

- ◆ **Debugging the source code**: You can inspect local variables, set watches, set breakpoints, and evaluate the code, live. You can also perform command-line debugging, and check the PHP output in the IDE without going to the browser, which provides competence for remote debugging.

- ◆ **Supporting PHP frameworks**: It also offers the support for popular PHP frameworks, such as the Zend Framework and Symfony.

 Comparison of integrated development environments for PHP can be found at `http://en.wikipedia.org/wiki/Comparison_of_integrated_development_environments#PHP`.

Recommended system requirements

Before we proceed with downloading the latest version, let's have a look into the recommended system requirements of various platforms for installing and running the NetBeans IDE:

- ◆ Microsoft Windows XP Professional SP3/Vista SP1/Windows 7 Professional:

  - ❏ **Processor**: 2.6 GHz Intel Pentium IV or equivalent
  - ❏ **Memory**: 2 GB
  - ❏ **Disk space**: 1 GB of free disk space

- Ubuntu 12.04:
  - **Processor**: 2.6 GHz Intel Pentium IV or equivalent
  - **Memory**: 2 GB
  - **Disk space**: 850 MB of free disk space

- Macintosh OS X 10.7 Intel:
  - **Processor**: Dual-Core Intel (32 or 64-bit)
  - **Memory**: 2 GB
  - **Disk space**: 850 MB of free disk space

Downloading the NetBeans IDE

NetBeans can be your daily IDE for development that will assist you in increasing your coding productivity. It is a free-of-cost, open source IDE, which can be downloadable for different technologies, including Java, C/C++, PHP, and so on, and platforms such as Windows, Linux, Mac OS X, or even OS-independent bundles. Moreover, you may download the IDE only for PHP technology, or for all technologies in an installer package.

Again, if you are already using the IDE for the development of Java, C/C++, and so on, then you may skip this download, and the installation section, and jump directly to the section named *Adding PHP as a plugin to an already existing NetBeans installation*.

Time for action – downloading the NetBeans IDE

Go through the following steps to download the NetBeans IDE:

1. Visit `http://netbeans.org/downloads/` in order to download the latest NetBeans release. The download page will automatically detect your computer's operating system, and will let you download the operating, system-specific installer.

Note that you can add or remove packs or plugins later, using the IDE's plugin manager. Also, you can select "OS-independent ZIP" if you want to avoid installation. Again, NetBeans is a must-have IDE for those programmers who work with multiple programming language platforms. Currently, NetBeans IDE supports various development platforms—J2SE, J2EE, J2ME, PHP, C/C++, and so on.

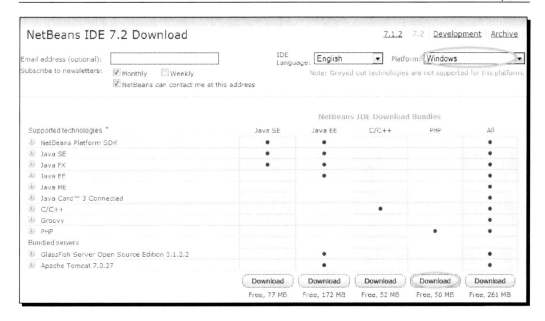

Next, we are going to download the PHP bundle, as shown in the screenshot above..

2. After clicking on the **Download** button, the page will be redirected to an auto download, along with a direct download link, as shown in the following screenshot:

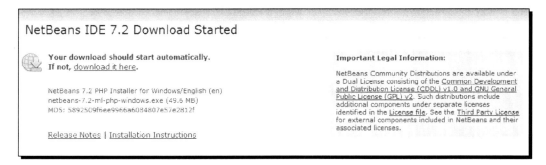

As you can see, your download starts automatically; Firefox users should see a window to save the file, which will appear as follows:

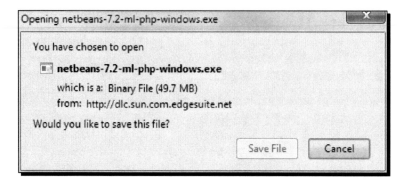

3. Save the file onto your disk space.

What just happened?

We just downloaded the installation file for the NetBeans PHP bundle. The PHP bundle provides tools for PHP 5.x development, and Zend and Symfony framework support. If you click on the **All** download option, you'll have the installation file for all mentioned technologies and during installation you will be able to choose exactly what tools and runtimes to install. So, now we are ready launch the installation wizard.

Installing NetBeans

Installing NetBeans is pretty much easier with the installation wizard, which guides the user with the required steps or configurations. Those who are already using NetBeans for other technologies, such as Java or C/C++, can skip this section and jump directly to the section named *Adding PHP as a plugin to an already existing NetBeans installation*.

 The PHP and C/C++ NetBeans bundles only require the **Java Runtime Environment (JRE) 6** to be installed. However, if you are planning to use any of the Java features, you need JDK 6 or JDK 7.

Time for action – installing NetBeans step by step

In this section, we will install the NetBeans IDE step by step, for Windows OS—that is, Windows 7. In order to install the software, you need to run the installer and proceed with the followings steps:

1. Run or execute the installer. The first step will look similar to the following screenshot:

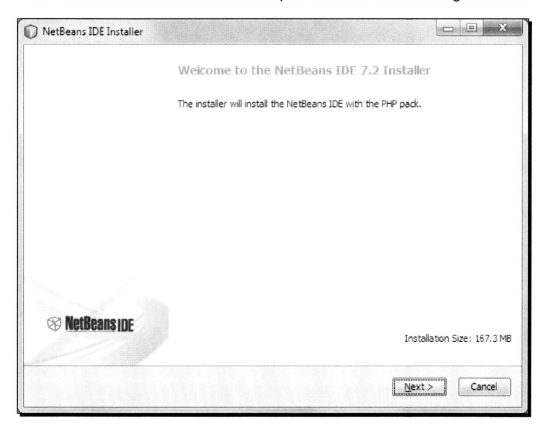

2. By clicking on the **Next** button, you will be asked to accept the license agreement:

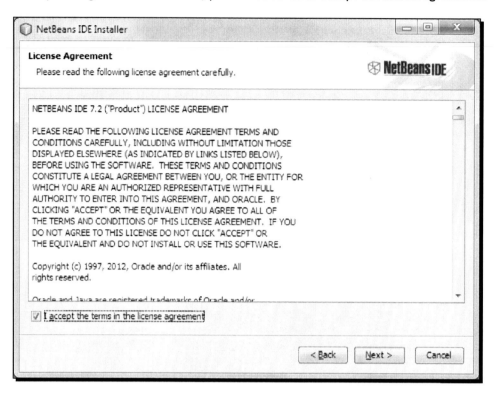

3. The next step will ask you for the installation location for NetBeans and the JRE, with some default program file path:

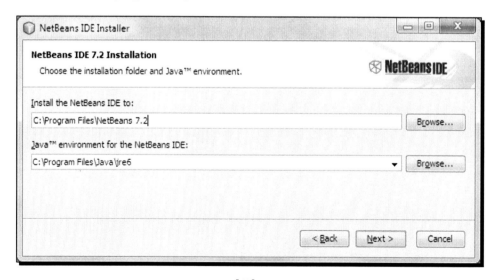

Note that JRE is the Java software for your computer, or the Java Runtime Environment, which is also referred to as the **Java Virtual Machine** (**JVM**). JRE will be installed as well.

4. Set the `installation` folder using the file browser, and click on the **Next** button. The next screenshot shows the total installation size:

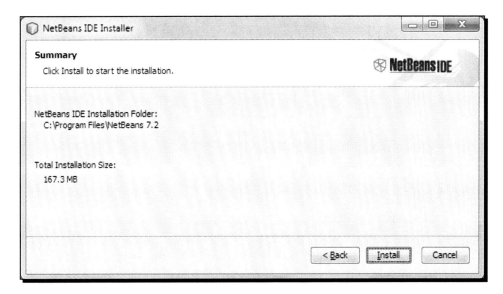

5. If everything is set, start the installation by clicking on the **Install** button, which will start the installation process.

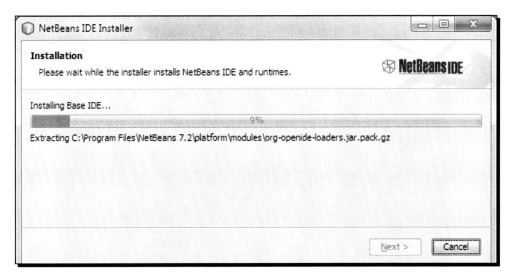

6. After everything is installed correctly, you will see the finish wizard, as shown in the following screenshot:

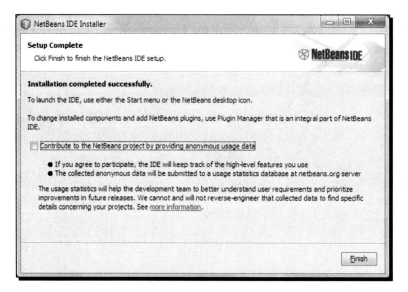

7. You may check or uncheck the **Contribute to the NetBeans project by providing anonymous usage data** checkbox, as per your wish to participate or not. Note that it will send project-specific usage data to netbeans.org, so read the on-screen instructions carefully before checking it. Complete the installation by clicking on the **Finish** button. Now, go to your OS's **Program** menu or into the directory where you have installed the IDE to be run. The IDE initializes with a splash screen, as shown below:

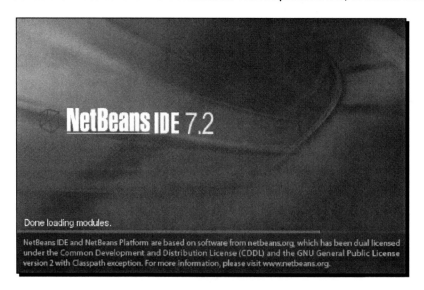

8. Finally, the running IDE looks similar to the following screenshot:

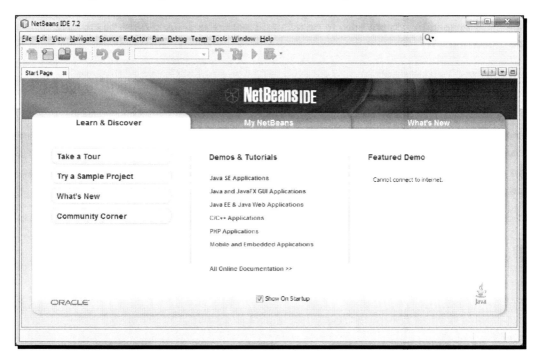

What just happened?

Now that we have the IDE up and running, we can go on to explore setting up the development environment with various operating systems.

In the next section, we will configure our PHP development environment on various operating systems. We will use the latest Apache-MySQL-PHP package installer, that is LAMP, XAMPP, and MAMP, for corresponding operating systems.

Adding PHP as a plugin to an already existing NetBeans installation

If you want to add functionality to your NetBeans IDE configuration, use the NetBeans Plugin Manager. For example, assume that you have already been running the NetBeans IDE for the Java or C/C++ pack. You then decide that you want to try out the PHP functionality. To do this, go to the NetBeans Plugin Manager from the IDE (choose **Tools | Plugins**), and add the PHP pack to your existing installation.

Multiple installation support

Multiple installations of NetBeans IDE 5.x, 6.x, and 7.x can coexist with the latest version on the same system. You do not have to uninstall the earlier versions in order to install or run the latest one.

If you have an earlier installation of the NetBeans IDE, you can choose whether or not to import the user settings from the existing user directory when you run the latest IDE for the first time.

Have a go hero – adding or removing features from NetBeans

So, you have NetBeans up and running on your computer. Now, add more features or remove unnecessary features, to or from your installed NetBeans, and check the newly added feature(s) inside the IDE. You may try the plugin manager to do this.

Setting up your development environment in Windows

Instead of installing and configuring Apache, MySQL, and PHP individually, we will use the XAMPP package to have all of them installed and configured automatically. We will download and install the latest XAMPP package (v. 1.7.7), which includes the following:

- Apache 2.2.21
- MySQL 5.5.16
- PHP 5.3.8
- phpMyAdmin 3.4.5
- FileZilla FTP Server 0.9.39

Time for action – installing XAMPP in Windows

The following steps will download and install the XAMPP package:

1. We will download the installer for the latest XAMPP package from:
   `http://www.apachefriends.org/en/xampp-windows.html`.

2. After completing the download, run the `.exe` file to proceed with the installation. More installation details can be found at:
   `http://www.apachefriends.org/en/xampp-windows.html`.

3. You will be given a choice to install the Apache server and the MySQL database server as services, so you don't need to start them manually from the XAMPP Control Panel. Again, you will have the option to configure those services, such as start/stop, run as service, and uninstall from the XAMPP control panel later.

4. After completing the installation process successfully, you will be able to proceed with further steps. Open the XAMPP control panel from your operating system's **Start | Programs | XAMPP**.

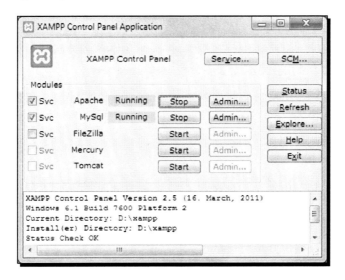

Svc checkboxes indicate that the module was installed as a Windows service, and hence will start with the Windows startup, or you can check them to be running as a service. If you ever need to restart your Apache web server, use the **Stop/Start** button besides **Status** of **Apache**.

5. Now, check your XAMPP installation. Visit the URL `http://localhost` from your web browser; the XAMPP welcome page looks similar to the following screenshot:

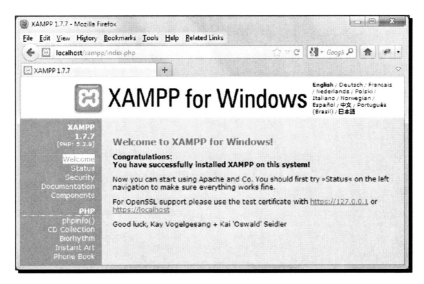

6. From the left, click `phpinfo()` to check the PHP release and the installed components that you have configured:

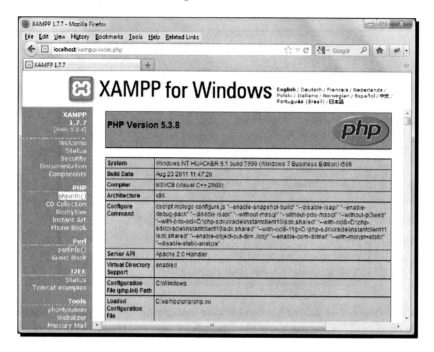

7. Click on the **Status** menu under the **Welcome** menu to check the installed tools status; the activated green status beside corresponding columns means that you are running Apache, MySQL, and PHP successfully:

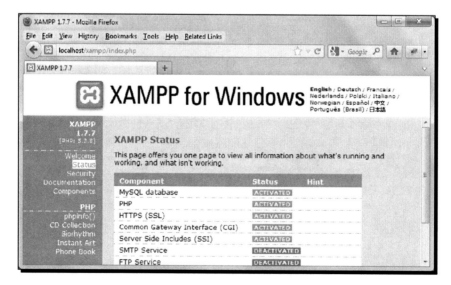

What just happened?

We have successfully installed and run the XAMPP package on our system. We have the XAMPP control panel in order to control the installed services and we also have a web interface to manage MySQL databases.

Have a go hero – securing your XAMPP installation

XAMPP is not meant for production use, but only for developers in a development environment. XAMPP is configured to be as open as possible, and it allows the web developers to fetch anything they want. For development environments, this is great. But, in a production environment, it could be fatal. So, you need to secure your XAMPP installation with the help of the *A matter of security* section, at `http://www.apachefriends.org/en/xampp-windows.html`.

> To display errors in the development environment, update the loaded `php.ini` file to set `display_errors = On`, and do the reverse `display_errors = Off` for the production environment.

Setting up your development environment in the Ubuntu desktop

Linux, **Apache**, **MySQL**, and **PHP** (**LAMP**) are some of the most common web hosting platforms. So, it's a perfect environment for you to build and test your website code. In this section, we will have our own LAMP set up, configured, and running easily into our Ubuntu 12.04 desktop.

Time for action – installing LAMP on the Ubuntu desktop

Follow the steps listed here in order to install the LAMP package in Ubuntu:

1. Instead of installing each item separately, we will go with installing the LAMP server in a package in Ubuntu, which is fairly simple, along with a single terminal command:

   ```
   sudo apt-get install lamp-server^
   ```

   The `apt-get` command is a powerful command-line tool, which is used to work with Ubuntu's **Advanced Packaging Tool** (**APT**) performing functions such as the installation of new software packages, upgrading the existing software packages, updating of the package list index, and even upgrading the entire Ubuntu system.

sudo, used to invoke the current user with the power of a super user and a caret (^) symbol, is placed after the package name to indicate that tasks are being performed together.

2. This command will cause the LAMP package to start installing immediately along with the latest PHP5, Apache 2, MySQL and PHP5-MySQL software. By default, Apache 2 and MySQL install as a service, and your document root will be at /var/www/, and an index.html file will be at /var/www/.

3. Both Apache and MySQL should be running. However, if required, you may start Apache by using the service start command as follows:

```
sudo service apache2 start
```

You can stop Apache by using the following command:

```
sudo service apache2 stop
```

4. Now, let's check the LAMP installation. Point your browser to http://localhost/, and you will see the default, Apache 2 landing page, as shown in the following screenshot:

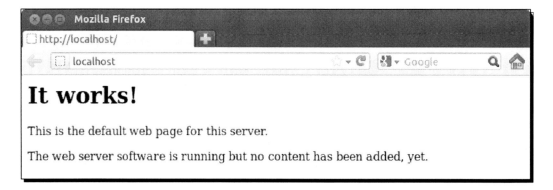

This means that your Apache 2 web server is running. You can still check these service statuses as follows:

```
sudo service apache2 status
```

The previous command will give you the following output:

```
Apache is running. Process #
```

5. Again, to check the MySQL status, simply run the following command:

```
sudo service mysql status
```

The following output will be displayed:

```
mysql start/running. Process #
```

6. To check the PHP installation, simply create a file named `test.php` in `/var/www/`, with the following line:

```
<?php phpinfo(); ?>
```

 You can create a new file from the terminal by using `touch test.php` or using gedit application, then editing the file, and saving it.

7. Now, point your browser to `http://localhost/test.php`, and you will see the installed PHP and the component's configuration details:

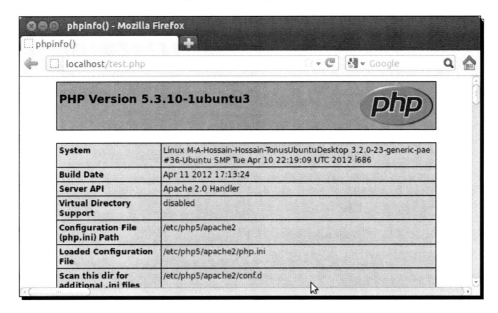

Steps 8 to *12* are optional, as we install `phpMyAdmin` in these steps.

8. Though we can maintain our databases using NetBeans, we still need to maintain the MySQL database functionalities using a web-based interface. To do this, we may use phpMyAdmin.

```
sudo apt-get install phpmyadmin
```

phpMyAdmin will be installed with this command, and during the installation, you will receive a blue window asking which server you want to use—apache2 or lighttpd. Choose apache2, and click on **OK** to continue with the installation. Note that during the installation, you may be asked to configure phpMyAdmin for database-config, passwords, and so on.

9. After the installation point, open your browser with http://localhost/phpmyadmin/, and you will be able to view a phpMyAdmin landing page, as shown in the following screenshot:

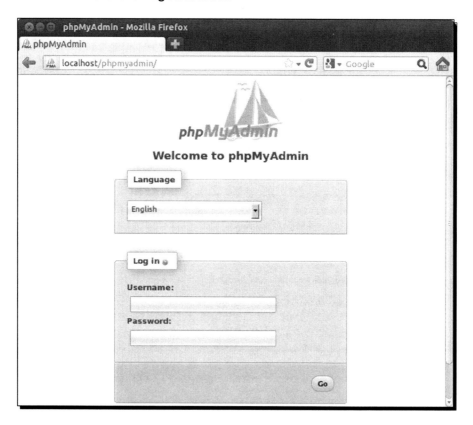

10. If you receive a `404` error at `http://localhost/phpmyadmin/`, then you need to manually set up `phpMyAdmin` under Apache, by modifying `/etc/apache2/apache2.conf` using `gedit` (the official text editor for the GNOME desktop):

```
sudo gedit /etc/apache2/apache2.conf
```

11. `gedit` will open the file in a graphical mode, and will add the following line inside `apache2.conf` at the bottom:

```
Include /etc/phpmyadmin/apache.conf
```

12. Now, restart the Apache server to make the changes effective:

```
sudo service apache2 restart
```

Refresh your browser, and you will now have the same `phpMyAdmin` login screen as shown in the previous screenshot.

What just happened?

The PHP development environment in the Ubuntu desktop has been set up successfully. The installation of the LAMP server was really a charm with a single command. We learned how to stop or restart services such as Apache and MySQL, along with checking their status.

Also, we have optionally installed `phpMyAdmin` for managing databases via the web interface. Note that `phpMyAdmin` is not meant for production use, but only for developers, in a development environment.

Have a go hero – displaying errors

As we have crafted our environment for development, PHP error messages will be very helpful for us to resolve them. By default, PHP error messages are turned off in your LAMP installation. You can enable the error messages displaying from the loaded `php.ini` file (see `phpinfo`) by modifying the line that contains `display_errors`. Note that any changes to `php.ini` requires the Apache 2 server to restart.

Setting up your development environment in Mac OS X

As we are interested in setting up AMP in a bundle, a MAMP package could be a good one for Mac OS X.

Time for action – installing MAMP in Mac OS X

Follow the steps below to download and install MAMP in your Mac OS X:

1. Download the latest MAMP release from `http://www.mamp.info/en/`; download MAMP by clicking on the **Download now** button under **MAMP package downloader**:

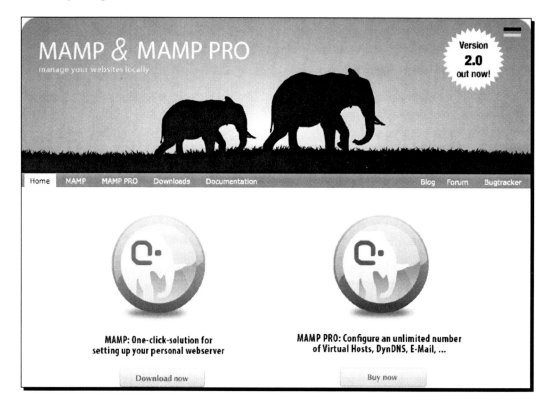

2. As shown in the preceding screenshot, choose the MAMP download on the left-hand side of the screen.

3. Extract the downloaded file, and run the `.dmg` file. After accepting the "terms of use", you will see a screen similar to the following:

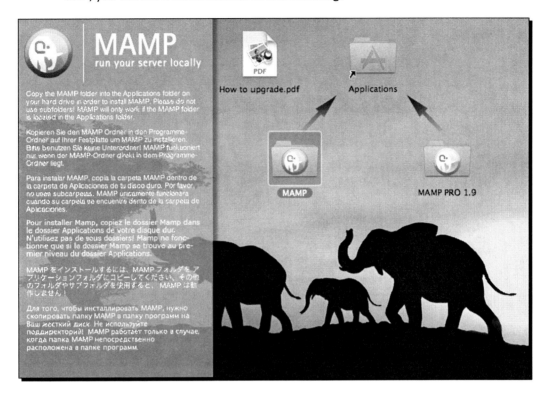

4. Drag the `MAMP` folder into the `Applications` folder; the MAMP installation is now complete on your Mac OS X.

5. Now, let's check our MAMP installation. Point your browser to `http://localhost/MAMP/`, and you will see the default MAMP landing page, as shown in the following screenshot:

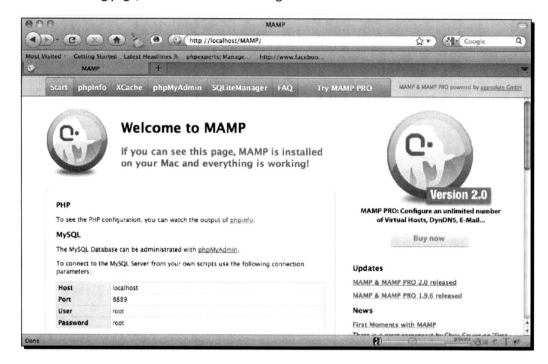

You can check **phpinfo**, **phpMyAdmin**, and so on, on the top bar at the **Start** page of MAMP.

6. From `/Applications/MAMP/`, double-click on `MAMP.app` to run the Apache, MySQL, PHP, and MAMP control panel. The **MAMP** control panel shows the server status, and lets you start/stop servers, as shown in the following screenshot:

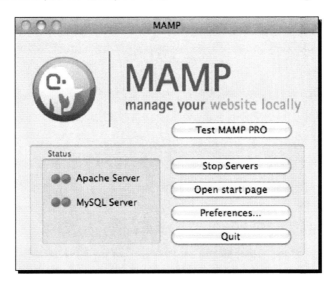

7. Switch to PHP version 5.3 from the MAMP control panel at **Preferences... | PHP Tab** (it requires a server restart).

What just happened?

We have successfully downloaded and installed MAMP for our Mac OS X development environment. Also, we have tested the installation, and found that it is up and running perfectly. The MAMP landing page comes with a tabbed interface, with `phpinfo`, `phpMyAdmin`, `SQLiteManager`, and so on. You have the following program and libraries installed with your MAMP bundle:

- Apache 2.0.63
- MySQL 5.1.44
- PHP 5.2.13 and 5.3.2
- APC 3.1.3
- eAccelerator 0.9.6
- XCache 1.2.2 and 1.3.0
- phpMyAdmin 3.2.5
- Zend Optimizer 3.3.9
- SQLiteManager 1.2.4

- Freetype 2.3.9
- t1lib 5.1.2
- curl 7.20.0
- jpeg 8
- libpng-1.2.42
- gd 2.0.34
- libxml 2.7.6
- libxslt 1.1.26
- gettext 0.17
- libidn 1.15
- iconv 1.13
- mcrypt 2.6.8
- YAZ 4.0.1 and PHP/YAZ 1.0.14

So far, we have installed the latest NetBeans IDE, and set up our platform-precise development environment with up-to-date Apache, MySQL, and PHP. Now, our recently completed development environment is well-crafted enough to start building projects. We will head for PHP project creation and maintenance with the help of IDE. Such a synergetic approach between the developer and the IDE can really improve productivity.

Have a go hero – securing your MAMP installation

As we have learned, MAMP is not meant for production use, but only for developers in a development environment. Secure your MAMP installation with the help of the MAMP forum at `http://forum.mamp.info/viewtopic.php?t=365`. You may need to set the MySQL password, `phpMyAdmin` password, secure the MAMP landing page, and so on.

Creating a NetBeans PHP project

NetBeans groups all of the necessary files for developing an application into a project. Project files consist of your original code along with any imported code that your project may be dependent on. NetBeans project management makes it easier to work on large projects by instantly showing you how a change in one part of the program will affect the rest of the program. So, the IDE provides features to facilitate the development growing through the project.

Time for action – creating a NetBeans PHP project

Finally, we are going to create a NetBeans PHP project to have the PHP content organized, and get more control over the created project.

In order to create a NetBeans PHP project, follow the steps below:

1. In order to start the project creation, go to **File | New Project** from the IDE menu bar.

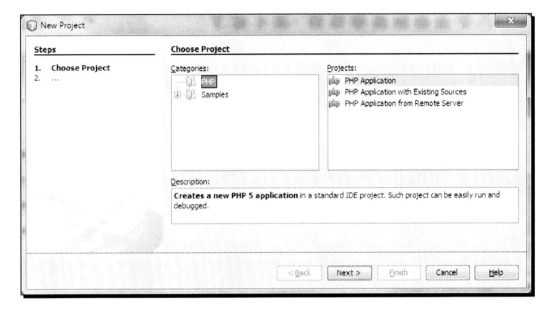

2. From this window, choose **PHP** for the project category, and select **PHP Application** that is selected by default, which means we are going to create a PHP project from scratch. If you already have source PHP code, then go for **PHP Application with Existing Sources**, and you will have to browse to your existing sources to set your source directory.

3. Click on the **Next** button, which will take you to the following screen, as shown below:

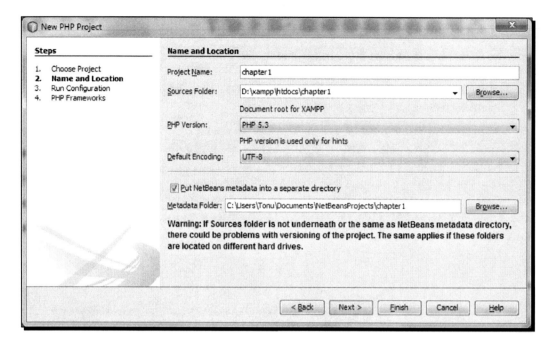

4. Define the project name and IDE, which automatically suggests the source folder for the given name. However, we can explicitly define the source folder path by browsing the folder path. Also, choose the appropriate **PHP Version**, according to which the project will behave at the IDE, and select **Default Encoding**. We will go for the selected items, by default, to have the latest PHP version behavior, and UTF-8 as **Default Encoding**.

5. Remember that the project metadata is the data that is used only at the local stage; optionally, you may put the project metadata created by NetBeans into a separate directory. To do that, check the box **Put NetBeans metadata into a separate directory**.

6. So, we name our project as `chapter1`, and click on **Next**, as shown in the following screenshot:

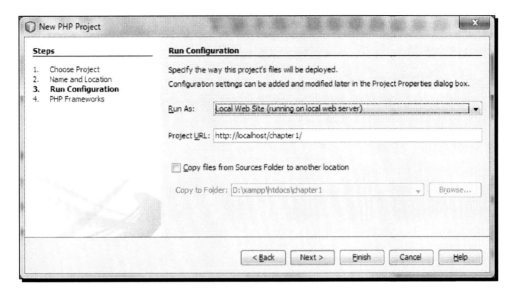

7. Define where the project will run (remote server, and so on), as well as the project URL. The default project URL is a formation of `http://localhost/` concatenated with a trailing project name. Click on **Next** to get to the following screenshot:

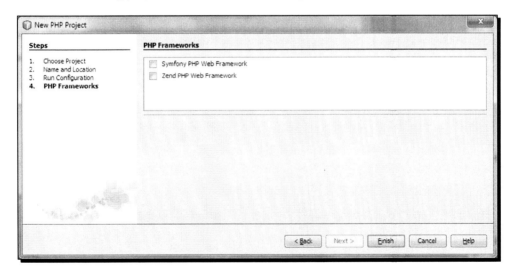

Optional checkboxes are used to add the PHP framework support into your project, if required. The IDE supports the two popular PHP frameworks—the Symfony and Zend frameworks.

8. Finally, click on **Finish** to complete the project wizard, and NetBeans will open the PHP project. It should look similar to the following screenshot:

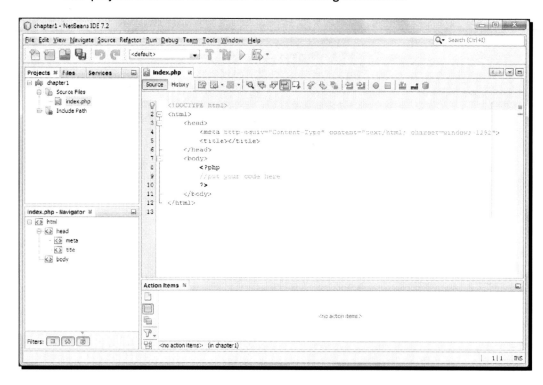

An index page, `index.php`, is created inside the project source automatically.

9. To test the project, we will put some code between PHP tags. So, let's put a simple `echo` as follows:

```php
<?php
echo "Hello World";
?>
```

10. Save the file and point your browser to a project URL, `http://localhost/chapter1/`. The page should give an output similar to the following screenshot:

So, we can see that our PHP project is performing fine.

11. To add more files and classes into our project, you may right-click on the project name, which will show the **Project** menu:

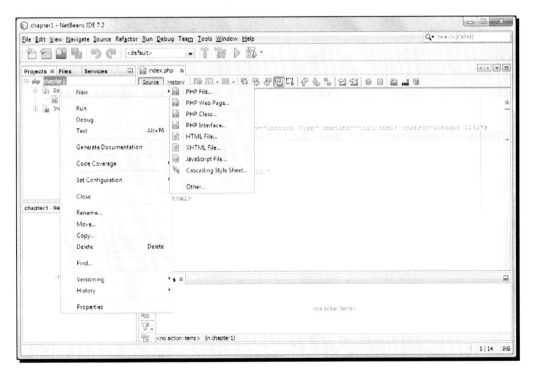

With this project context menu, we can add more PHP files, classes, and so on from **New**, whenever required. As we can see in this screenshot, a project can be modified as well. For example, you can rename, copy, or alter the project configuration, should you so wish.

What just happened?

Creating a new PHP project in NetBeans has worked like a charm. While creating it, we have observed that we can easily set several configurations of a project with the help of the step-by-step project creation wizard. Also, we have seen that after the creation of a new project, the IDE supports new PHP files, classes, interfaces, and so on from the project context menu. Note that, from the project context menu, you can manage the project operations, such as running and versioning tasks. To change the settings of an existing project, position the cursor on the project node, and choose **Properties** from the pop-up menu.

So, from now on, these will be our steps to create a new PHP project in NetBeans.

Have a go hero – creating a project from existing sources

If you already have some foundation source code for a PHP project, you can bring those source files under NetBeans, to have more control over the project. Create a new project from existing sources by selecting **File | New Project**.

Summary

We have practiced setting up the development environment for a particular operating system. We have the IDE, web server, database server, scripting language, and database management web interface installed and running successfully.

Specifically, we covered:

- ◆ NetBeans IDE installation
- ◆ PHP development environment setup on various platforms
- ◆ Creating a PHP project in NetBeans IDE

We also discussed the importance of using such IDEs, and how we could benefit from the IDE. Now that we've all the necessary kits to start PHP development, in the next chapter we will learn about the editor features to do fast and productive PHP development.

2
Boosting Your Coding Productivity with the PHP Editor

In this chapter, we shall discuss how to increase our coding productivity using the editor, and how to get the most out of the NetBeans Editor.

We shall focus on the following:

- The base IDE features
- The editor for PHP
- Rename refactoring and instant rename
- Code completion
- Code generators

So let's get on with it...

Familiarizing yourself with the base IDE features

As an IDE, NetBeans supports a wide range of features to boost your daily PHP development. It includes the editor, debugger, profiler, version control, and other collaborative features. The base IDE provides the following interesting features:

- **Quick search**: NetBeans provides you with a searching facility throughout the IDE, such as search within files, types, symbols, menu actions, options, help and open projects, Press *Ctrl+I* to focus on the search box. In the search results list, you will find the typed search term highlighted among the resultant items:

- **Plugin manager**: From **Tools | Plugins**, you will have the plugin manager from where you can add, remove, or update features. Also, many interesting third-party plugins are available from the plugin portal. Note that from the installed plugin's list, you can deactivate or uninstall plugins (CVS, Mercurial, and so on), which are not of your concern right now, but you may do that to free some resources, and add back those plugins whenever you want:

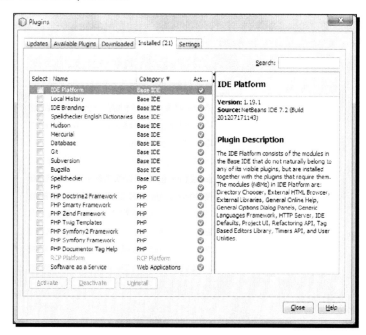

◆ **Project manager**: From **Window | Projects** or by pressing *Ctrl+1*, you can fix the **Project Manager** pane of the IDE to perform operations on each of the available projects. Project operations, such as run, debug, test, generate documentation, check local history, set configuration, and set project properties can all be done at the project manager window:

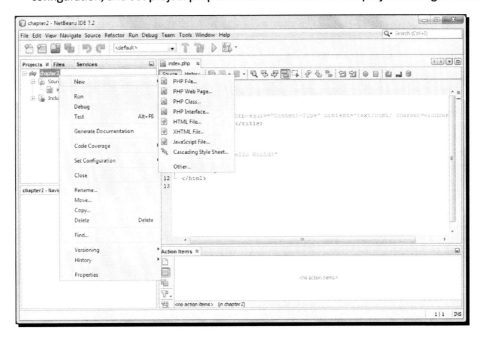

◆ **File manager**: From **Window | Files** or by pressing *Ctrl+2*, you can fix the **File Manager** pane of the IDE to browse project files or to manipulate general file operations on the files available to the IDE:

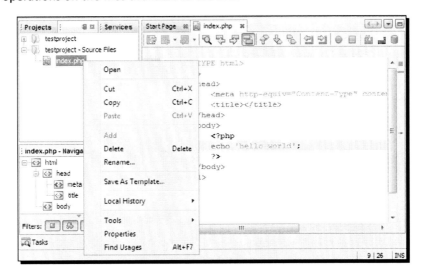

♦ **Services manager**: From **Window | Services** or by pressing *Ctrl+5*, you can fix the **Services Manager** pane of the IDE to use the pre-registered **Software as a Service (SaaS)** web-service components. Drag the item from the **Services** tab, drop the item in the resource class, and you will have the necessary code generated to access the service. Also, the **Services** pane gives you access to all your connected databases:

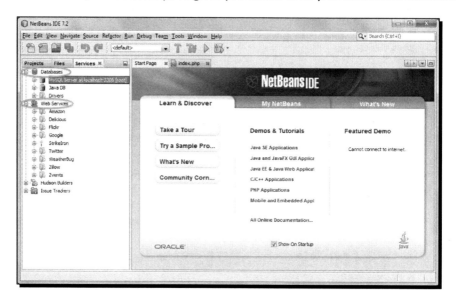

♦ **Task manager**: From **Window | Tasks** or by pressing *Ctrl+6*, you can fix the **Tasks Manager** or Action Items pane of the IDE. NetBeans IDE automatically scans your code and lists the commented lines containing words, such as TODO or FIXME, and lines with compile errors, quick fixes, and style warnings. Connect to a bug database—**Bugzilla**, and list issue reports for your project right in the IDE. Note that double-clicking on a task will take you straight to where it has been declared:

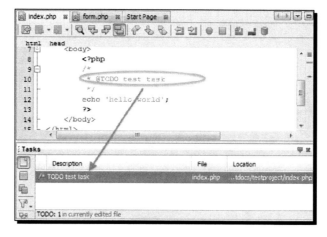

◆ **Navigate**: From the **Navigate** menu, the IDE provides navigation to a file, type, symbol, line, bookmark, and so on. Such features are used for a quick jump over the desired location in the project, or outside of it:

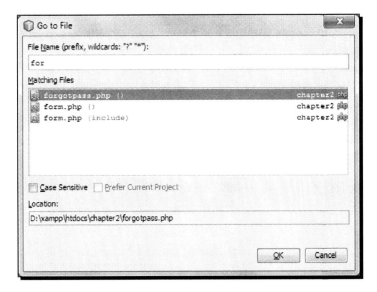

As shown in the previous screenshot, as soon as we type in the filename, the IDE shows a dynamic list of matched file names in the **Matching Files** box, so that you can quickly open that file:

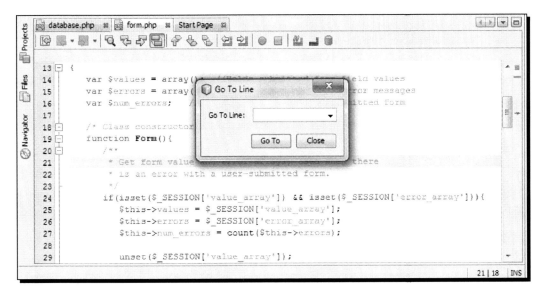

Press *Alt+Shift+O* to open **Go to file**, *Ctrl+O* to open **Go to type**, *Ctrl+B* to open **Go to declaration**, *Ctrl+G* to open **Go to line**, and so on.

- **Templates and sample applications**: You can start a similar new project with the given sample applications in the IDE. To do this, start a new project by pressing *Ctrl+Shift+N* and choose **Samples | PHP** from **Project Categories**. Also, you may use templates, such as the templates of PHP files, and web pages from **Tools | Templates**:

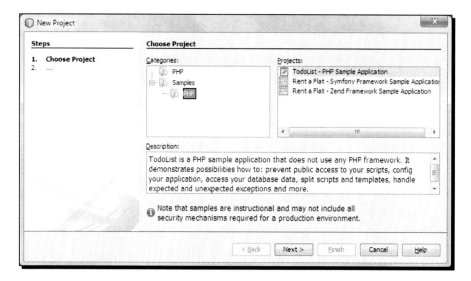

- **Customizable workspace and windows**: The entire IDE workspace is fully customizable, so that you can drag, slide, resize, and place toolbars & panes to your desired place. Also, you can dock or undock panes at your workspace, to make it fully comfortable for access and use:

You can manage windows in your workspace easily; double-click on an editor tab to expand it. *Ctrl+Tab* shows the opened file's list, and pressing it again will cause it to switch between the editor tabs. *Ctrl+Pageup/Down* switches among the opened files. Press *Ctrl+W* to close the current file window.

◆ **Multiple monitors**: You can undock any editor tab and drag it outside the IDE, so that it can act like an independent window, and you can easily move it to a second screen. Also, you can reverse the procedure to dock it back again in the previous screen. Note that all of the shortcuts will remain the same in the second screen; for example, drag out the **Files** tab and click anywhere else in the IDE, and then press *CTRL+2* to regain focus on the files window.

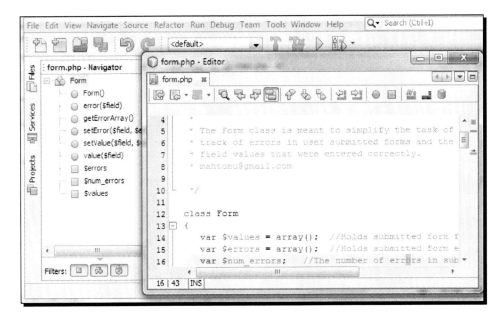

◆ **Local history**: Local history is similar to a classic versioning system in which it stores multiple versions of files. However, the storage is only local to your NetBeans installation. Local history enables you to examine the content within files and folders on time, lets you **diff** them, and most importantly, lets you roll back your sources to some previous state, or revert already deleted files or folders.

◆ **Spellchecker**: Spellcheck the text in the editor.

 See the Appendix for NetBeans IDE keyboard shortcuts.

Pop quiz – familiarizing yourself with basic IDE features

1. Which is not an IDE feature?
   a. Source code editor
   b. Debugger
   c. Plugin manager
   d. Source code optimizer

2. Under which menu can all the IDE windows be enabled or focused?
   a. File menu
   b. Tools menu
   c. Navigate menu
   d. Windows menu

3. Which is the correct command to open the **Go to a File** window?
   a. CTRL+F
   b. CTRL+SHIFT+O
   c. ALT+SHIFT+O
   d. CTRL+G

4. Why is the keyboard shortcut *CTRL+SHIFT+N* used?
   a. To open a new template file
   b. To open a new PHP file
   c. To open a new PHP project
   d. To open the Project window

5. What is the keyboard shortcut to fix the **File manager** pane?
   a. CTRL+1
   b. CTRL+2
   c. CTRL+3
   d. CTRL+5

Exploring the editor for PHP

In this section, we will learn how to get the most out of the editor for PHP in NetBeans. The editor provides very handy code-authoring features, and we shall learn those important features by testing them in our editor. Once we are familiar with the following features, we will rule the editor. All you have to do is just practice the commands mentioned for the following features. Here we go:

- **Syntax highlighting**: This editor enables the highlighting of syntax elements, such as PHP keywords, variables, constants, HTML tags, and input form attributes. In the editor, the current line is marked with a light blue background, and the line where any error occurred is displayed with a red underline, as shown in the following screenshot:

```php
function Form(){
    /**
     * Get form value and error arrays, used when there
     * is an error with a user-submitted form.
     */
    if(isset($_SESSION['value_array']) && isset($_SESSION['error_array'])){
        $this->values = $_SESSION['value_array'];
        $this->errors = $_SESSION['error_array'];
        $this->num_errors = count($this->errors);

        unset($_SESSION['value_array'])
        unset($_SESSION['error_array']);
    }
    else{
        $this->num_errors = 0;
    }
}
```

 Double-click to select a syntax element. Press *Ctrl+F* for syntax searching to highlight all the occurrences of the syntax element.

◆ **Go To Declaration**: The **Go To Declaration** feature provides an instant jump to the line where a variable or method has been declared from its occurrence:

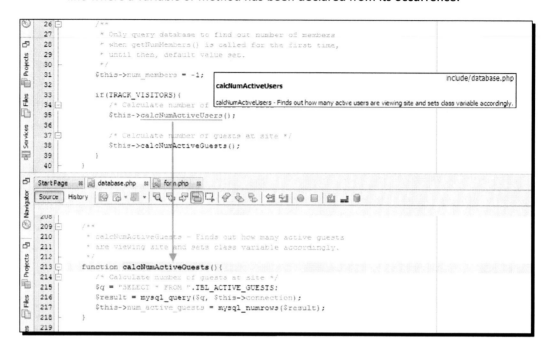

In order to use this feature, place the cursor on a desired variable or method, and press *Ctrl+B*, or click on the context menu that appeared on the right-hand side of the screen, choose **Navigate | Go to Declaration** to have your cursor placed at the start of the line where it was declared. Pressing *Ctrl*+left-click will also direct you to the declaration, along with all the occurrences that are highlighted.

◆ **Code navigator**: The **Code navigator** pane dynamically lists the in-file PHP structure, HTML tags in hierarchical order; simply, it lists the namespaces, functions, methods, classes, variables, class properties, HTML tags, and so on within the file. Double-click on any item on the list to go to that declaration:

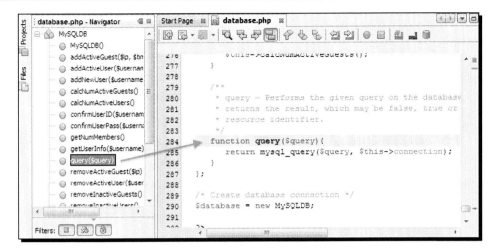

 From **Window | Navigating | Navigator** or by pressing *Ctrl+7*, you can focus on the code navigator pane. The listed items are iconized according to relevant item properties.

◆ **Code folding**: The editor provides you with the code block fold/unfold feature for classes, methods, comment blocks, HTML tags, CSS style classes, and so on. You can fold/unfold large code blocks using such features, right beside the left margin of the editor, as shown in the following screenshot:

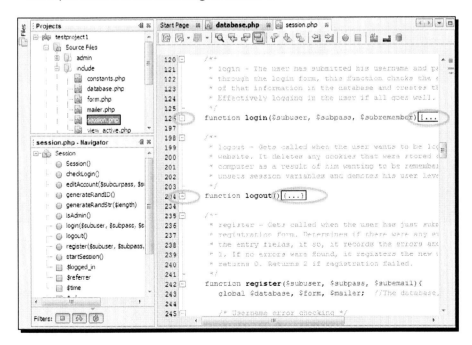

Click on the "−" or "+" button from the left side of the screen to fold and unfold code blocks.

◆ **Smart indent**: The editor provides an automatic indentation before the code, while typing and hitting on new lines:

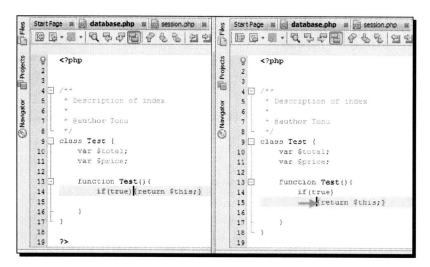

Type an `if` or `for` statement line, and press *Enter* to see the next line indented.

◆ **Formatting**: To make the code more understandable, the editor provides you with a formatting facility, which maintains appropriate statement hierarchy and applies line breaks, spaces, indents, and so on within the code file:

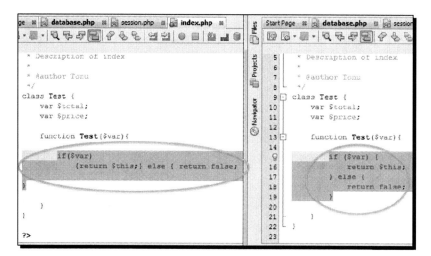

Select the code block you want to format. Right-click on the context menu, choose **Format**, or press *Alt+Shift+F*. To format the entire code file, choose **Source | Format**, or press *Ctrl+A* and *Alt+Shift+F*.

◆ **Bracket completion**: The consecutive second character of the paired characters item such as single quotes (' '), double quotes (" "), braces (( )), and brackets ([ ]) are automatically added with the first character type, and the paired consecutive character is removed with the first one deleted again. Also, the pair of curly brackets ({ }) is completed when the first character is typed, and *Enter* is pressed. A pair of braces, curly braces, and brackets are highlighted with the yellow color when any of the characters from matching pairs are pointed at with the cursor, as follows:

◆ **Parameter hints**: The editor prompts you to choose the formal parameters of a PHP default or custom function just as soon as you start typing that function name. The automatic suggestion list with the function names and parameters will show at the bottom of the cursor, and the description of that selected function will show at the top of the cursor:

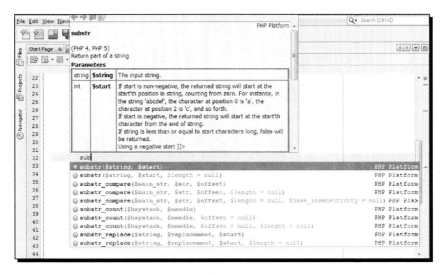

In the previous auto-suggestion list, you may traverse using the *Up/Down* arrow keys. You can hit *Enter* to insert the desired function name with the placeholders, to insert the parameters within the brackets:

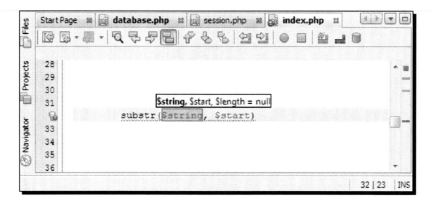

◆ **Defining a variable type in comments**: You can define a variable and its type in comments, in the format /* @var $variable type */. The var tag will be in bold font, if the comment was written correctly:

```php
<?php

class Student{
    function getName(){}
    function getId(){}
}

class Employer{
    function getCompany(){}
    function getEmployeeNo(){}
}

/* @var $std Student */
$std->
    getId()      Student
    getName() Student
```

```php
<?php

class Student{
    function getName(){}
    function getId(){}
}

class Employer{
    function getCompany(){}
    function getEmployeeNo(){}
}

/* @var $emp Employer */
$emp->
    getCompany()      Employer
    getEmployeeNo() Employer
```

In the previous screenshots, you can see how the comment for variable name and type dominates the auto suggestion. In the previous example, you can see that method names have been picked from the corresponding class name, mentioned as a variable type in the comment.

Type vdoc, and press *Tab* to use the code template for the variable documentation. A comment will be generated, which defines a variable. Once the variable name is selected, change it, and press *Tab* again, to change the type:

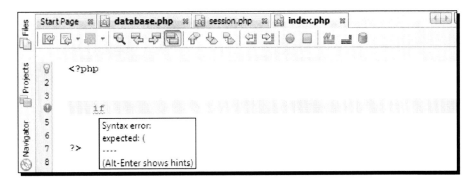

The code template automatically generates a variable name and type in the context of a comment position; that is, if you use the template just before the variable was used, then it will suggest that variable name and type.

◆ **Error messages**: The editor parses your PHP code while typing, marks the syntax errors with a red underline, places a red error bullet in the left margin, and a red error scroll position in the right margin.

You can see the error details in a tool tip, by hovering over the erroneous line or by clicking on the red error bullet on the left side of the screen. Press *Alt+Enter* to show error hints.

See the Appendix for NetBeans IDE keyboard shortcuts.

Pop quiz – exploring the editor for PHP

1. Which functionality is not an editor feature?

    a. Source code formatting

    b. Code auto completion

    c. Syntax highlighting

    d. Debugging

2. How do you format a code block?

    a. Select the code block by right-clicking on the context menu, and choose **Format**

    b. Select the code block and press *ALT+SHIFT+F*

    c. Select the code block and choose **Source | Format**

    d. All of the above

3. What is the syntax-searching keyboard command?

    a. *CTRL+W*

    b. *CTRL+F*

    c. *CTRL+ALT+F*

    d. *CTRL+SHIFT+S*

4. How to go to the declaration of a method?

    a. Place the cursor on the method and press *CTRL+B*

    b. Right-click on the method name, and choose **Navigate | Go to Declaration** from the context menu

    c. Press *CTRL*+left-click on the method name

    d. All of the above

Exploring more with the editor

We have learned about the editor and practiced the shortcuts given as tips. In the next two sections, we will learn to use the rename refactoring, code completion, and code generator features of the editor, which are really helpful to boost coding.

In the next section, we will discuss and practice the following important editor features:

◆ Rename refactoring and instant rename

◆ Code completion

◆ Code generators

Using rename refactoring and instant rename

You can rename an element, such as a class name, across all files in a project. This feature enables you to preview the possible changes in every location for that desired rename, and you can exclude individual occurrences from being renamed.

Instant rename lets you rename an element within a file. For instant rename, place the cursor on the name you want to rename, and press *Ctrl+R*; if instant rename is applicable to that variable, then all the instances of that variable are highlighted as follows:

```
123         * of that information in the database and creates the session.
124         * Effectively logging in the user if all goes well.
125        */
126 ⊟   function login($subuser, $subpass, $subremember){
127         global $database, $form;   //The database and form object
128
129 ⊟      /* Username error checking */
130         $field = "user";   //Use field name for username
131         if(!$subuser || strlen($subuser = trim($subuser)) == 0){
132             $form->setError($field, "* Username not entered");
133         }
134         else{
```

A change in even one instance of that name will rename all other instances in the file simultaneously:

```
123        * of that information in the database and creates the session.
124        * Effectively logging in the user if all goes well.
125        */
126 ⊟    function login($user, $subpass, $subremember){
127          global $database, $form;   //The database and form object
128
129 ⊟        /* Username error checking */
130          $field = "user";   //Use field name for username
131          if(!$user || strlen($user = trim($user)) == 0){
132              $form->setError($field, "* Username not entered");
133          }
134          else{
135 ⊟            /* Check if username is not alphanumeric */
```

To use rename refactoring, select the element to rename, then right-click, and select **Refactor | Rename**. A dialog box opens for you to rename the element, as shown in the next screenshot:

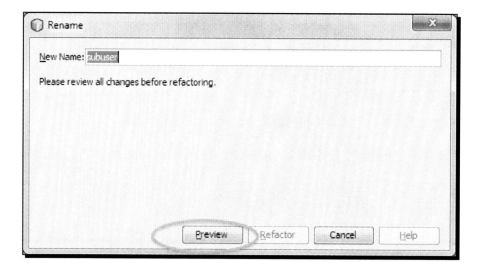

In this screenshot, provide a new name for the element and click on **Preview**. The refactoring window opens with all the instances of the element listed within the project:

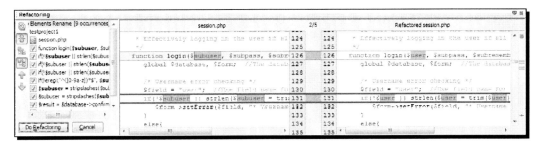

From this screenshot, you can exclude the instances and apply **Do Refactoring** to the selected instances.

 See the Appendix for NetBeans IDE keyboard shortcuts.

Pop quiz – using rename refactoring and instant rename

1. How do you refactor a variable name throughout the project?
   a. Select the variable, then right-click and select **Refactor | Rename**
   b. Place the cursor on the variable name, and press *CTRL+SHIFT+R*
   c. Select the variable, and select **Source | Rename**
   d. None of the above

2. Which is the shortcut on a variable for instant rename?
   a. *SHIFT+ALT+R*
   b. *CTRL+R*
   c. *CTRL+ALT+R*
   d. *CTRL+SPACE+R*

Using code completion

The code completion feature enables us to complete the desired syntax, methods, or code with some minimal keystrokes, or just with a keyboard command.

 You can enable/disable automatic code completion from **Tools | Options | Editor | Code Completion**. By default, you will have checkboxes for all languages. Choose PHP from the **Language** drop-down list to have more PHP-specific code completion options.

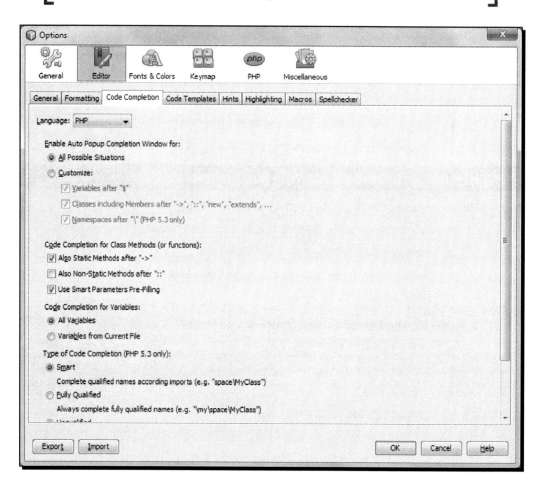

Following are the code completion features provided by the editor:

◆ **Snippets**: This automatically generates code snippets for various elements.

Select **Tools | Pallete | PHP Code Clips**, and **Pallete Manager** will open. Drag the relevant item icon from **Pallete Content**, and drop it to the relevant position in your code. A dialog box will appear for specifying the parameters of the corresponding code item. Fill in the parameters, and have the code generated in that place.

◆ **Context-sensitive proposals**: The editor provides context-sensitive proposals for any number of starting symbols for:

   ❏ A PHP keyword, including `if`, `else`, `elseif`, `while`, `switch`, `function` and so on.

   ❏ A PHP built-in function.

   ❏ A pre-defined or user-defined variable.

Type the starting characters of a keyword or a function name, and press *Ctrl+Space* bar. A drop-down list will show all the applicable proposals for that context. Each proposal is supplied with a description and parameter hints:

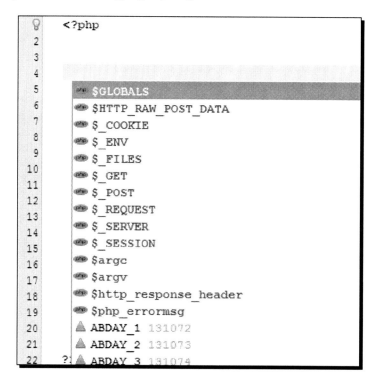

To generate a list of PHP keywords, which is applicable in the current context, press *Ctrl+Space* bar without typing anything:

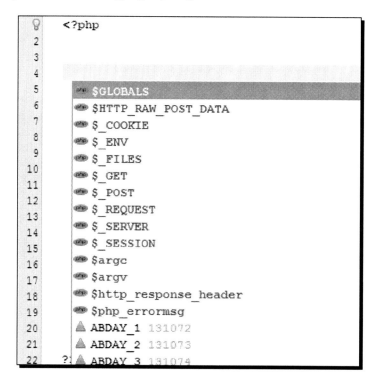

To obtain a hint on a variable, type the dollar ($) symbol. A list of currently-available local and global variables will be displayed:

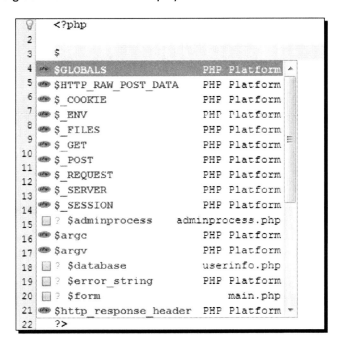

◆ **Code templates and abbreviations**: This obtains the expanded code template by using defined abbreviations of that template, such as `cls` for a class template, and is the most interesting code-completion feature. To use this functionality, type the abbreviation and press *Tab*:

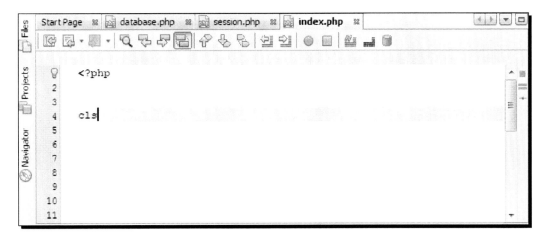

You can see that the abbreviation is replaced with the corresponding PHP keyword, and the code template for that keyword has been provided by the editor, as per the following screenshot:

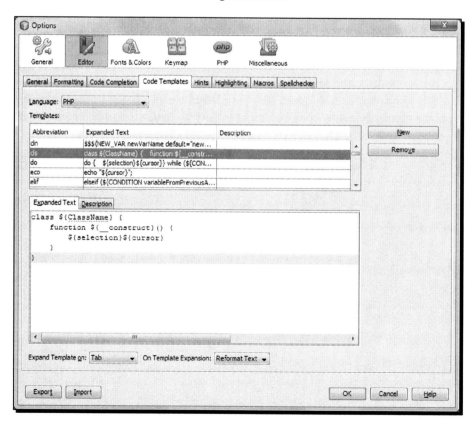

To view the list of code templates with their associated abbreviations, Select **Tools | Options | Editor | Code Templates**. You can add/remove or edit your PHP code templates as shown in the following screenshot:

Note that coding methods change over time. So, it is recommended to have a look into your templates every few months, and update them to comply with any new changes.

◆ **Code completion in constructors**: After the `new` keyword, code completion is displayed along with the list of constructors and parameters for all the classes available in the current project:

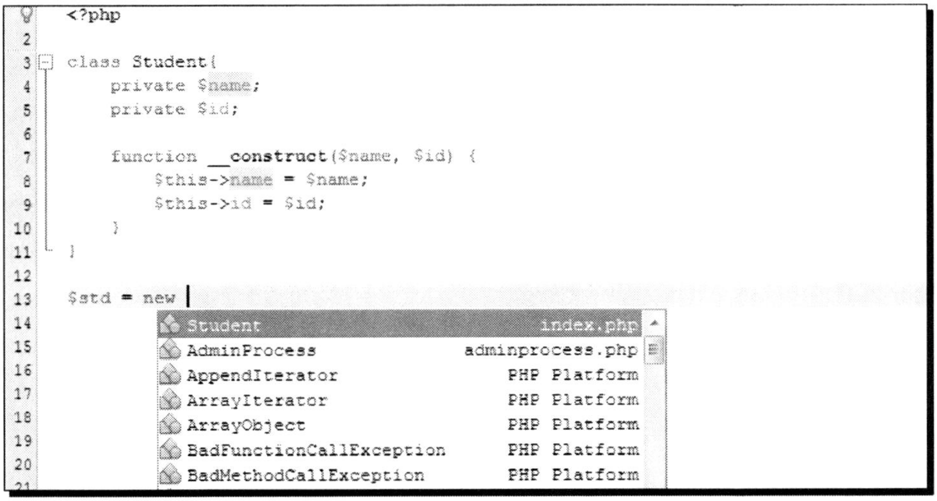

```php
<?php

class Student{
    private $name;
    private $id;

    function __construct($name, $id) {
        $this->name = $name;
        $this->id = $id;
    }
}

$std = new |
            Student                     index.php
            AdminProcess         adminprocess.php
            AppendIterator           PHP Platform
            ArrayIterator            PHP Platform
            ArrayObject              PHP Platform
            BadFunctionCallException PHP Platform
            BadMethodCallException   PHP Platform
```

◆ **SQL code completion**: When a string begins with SQL keywords such as `select` and `insert`, pressing *Ctrl+Space* after that keyword enables the SQL code-completion feature inside the editor. You can select the database connection in the first step, as shown in the following screenshot:

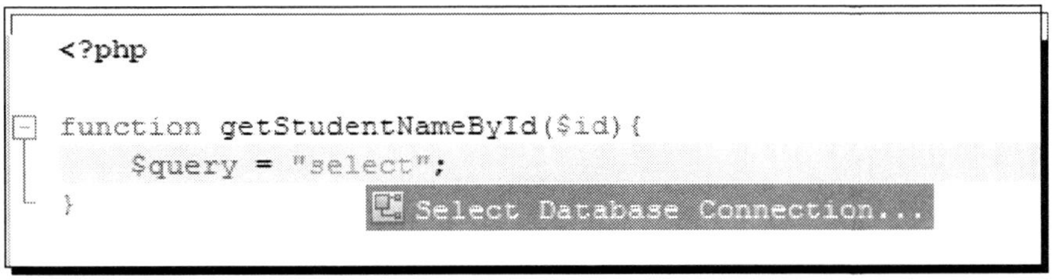

```php
<?php

function getStudentNameById($id){
    $query = "select";
                    Select Database Connection...
}
```

Along with being selected, all the database connections registered with the IDE will be displayed as follows:

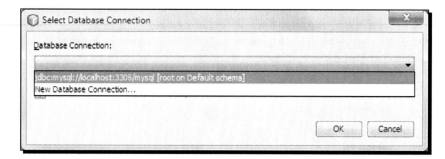

After selecting the database connection, the SQL code completion feature offers all the tables associated with that connection:

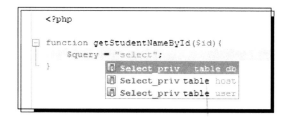

Also, the list of columns (if any) will be displayed from that table. SQL code completion also works with table aliases.

◆ **PHP 5.3 namespaces**: Code completion supports PHP 5.3 namespaces.

◆ **Overridden and implemented methods**: Code completion between class members offers to override or implement methods.

 Press *Ctrl+Space* bar wherever you wish to use code completion. See the Appendix for NetBeans IDE keyboard shortcuts.

Pop quiz – using code completion

1. Why is the code completion feature used?

    a. To refactor a variable

    b. To write a new PHP class

    c. To complete the desired syntax, methods, or code

    d. To complete a PHP project

2. Which PHP language feature does the code completion feature not support?

    a. Namespace

    b. Class declaration

    c. Override methods

    d. None of the above

3. What is the shortcut to enable the context-sensitive proposal?

    a. Ctrl+Shift+Space

    b. Ctrl+Space

    c. Ctrl+S

    d. Ctrl+Alt+Space

Using the code generator

The editor provides context-sensitive code generators, so as to generate a database connection, constructors, getters or setters, and so on. A specific code generator will appear in the context of cursor location. For example, inside a class, it will display for generating constructors, getters, setters, and so on.

As an example, press *Alt+Insert* inside a class to open all possible code generators, as shown in the following screenshot:

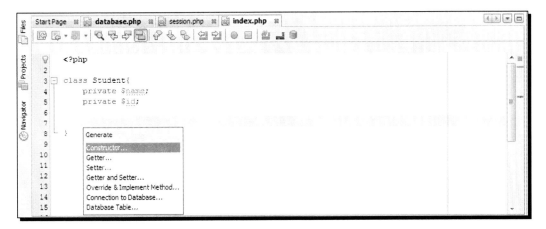

We will discuss the following code generators:

- ◆ **Constructors**: Inside a PHP class (but not inside any method's body), you can open the constructor generator by pressing *Alt+Insert*. Select **Generate Constructor**, and a dialog box similar to the following screenshot will appear:

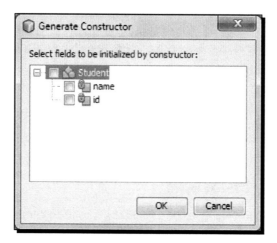

The window comes with a list of available fields that you can initialize in the constructor. Field names are used as parameters of the constructor. You can decide not to select any fields; an empty constructor will be generated in such a case.

- ◆ **Getters and setters**: By pressing the code generator command inside a PHP class, you can choose **Getters…**, **Setters…**, or **Getters and Setters** to view the possible functions. If you already have setters, then you will only view the getter methods:

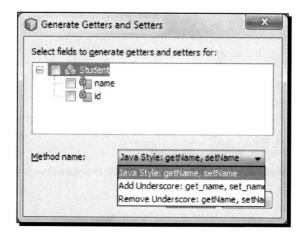

After selecting **getters/setters** the previous screenshot appears; you can specify for which property you want to generate a **getter** or a **setter** method, with a flexibility of choosing the naming convention for the method.

♦ **Overridden and implemented methods**: You can open the code generator for overridden and implemented methods when there are multiple methods inside the class. A dialog box opens, showing the methods you can insert, and indicates whether they are overridden or implemented:

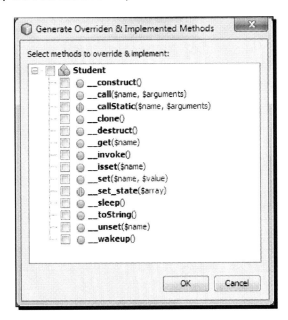

 See the *Appendix* for NetBeans IDE keyboard shortcuts.

Pop quiz – using code generators

1. What is the shortcut to open the code generator inside a PHP class?

    a. Alt+Insert

    b. Shift+Alt+Insert

    c. Ctrl+ Alt+Insert

    d. Ctrl+Insert

2. What cannot be generated using code generator?

    a. Constructors

    b. Getters and setters

    c. Overridden methods

    d. Strings

Summary

In this chapter, we have discovered useful features of the PHP editor, and practiced the tips to apply while code writing. Familiarization with the editor shortcuts we have looked at will help you to write the code faster and correctly.

We have especially focused on:

- The PHP editor features and shortcuts
- Rename refactoring and instant rename
- Usage of code completion
- Usage of code generators

So, up to now, we have our PHP development environment ready. We have installed the IDE, and learned how to use those cool editor features when required. In the next chapter, we will dive straight into real-life PHP coding, and will develop a PHP project to have a grip over web application development using NetBeans.

3
Building a Facebook-like Status Poster using NetBeans

In this chapter, we are going to build a cool PHP project using NetBeans IDE. Our plan is straightforward and simple.

We will be creating a Facebook-like status poster through the following steps:

- ◆ Planning the project
- ◆ Creating a status stream display list
- ◆ Creating a status poster using PHP-AJAX

Most of the social networking platforms, such as Facebook, Twitter, and Google Plus, provide a status-posting feature among a user's friends, and also let the user view their friends' status posts. So, we will snoop around on how this works and how we can build alike. Let's choose to implement an interesting feature similar to the most popular social networking platform—Facebook.

Also, we will discuss MySQL database connection and PHP class creation along with our workflow. So, let's go for it...

Planning the project

Proper planning of a project is crucial for the smart development and use of mockups, diagrams, and flow charts, so that the project can visualize the requirements easily. Moreover, it depicts what you are going to do, and how.

We will create a simple Facebook-like (`http://www.facebook.com`) status poster, and add a list below it to display the status posts from friends, as well as your own statuses. In this single, frontend PHP application, we will exercise the JavaScript library **jQuery** (`http://jquery.com/`) to post the status with **AJAX** (`http://api.jquery.com/jQuery.ajax/`). The posted status will be displayed on top of the status stack without reloading the page.

While planning our project, we will view the final look of the web application in advance, and try to understand how we can place a particular functionality to work. To discuss various points of the workflow, we will have the workflow diagram as well.

Let's have a look at what we will be building in the final stage.

This **Status Poster** will be functional in the following fashion:

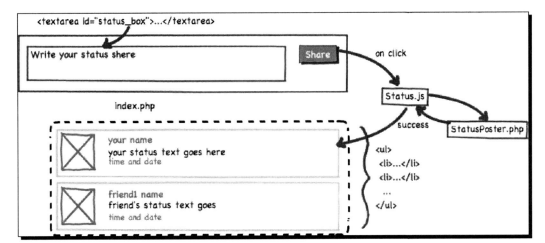

According to this figure, the user types in the status box and clicks on the **Share** button to trigger the bound JavaScript method inside `Status.js`, to post the status via AJAX to the server. The server-side script, `StatusPoster.php`, receives the status to save into the database, and responds with a success message after accomplishing the task. The frontend code receives the success notification and prepends the status at the top of the status post's display stack.

Now, we will break the project into two parts as follows, and will develop them accordingly:

◆ Status stream display list
◆ Status poster using PHP-AJAX

We have gathered concepts regarding project workflow. So, we can start implementing the project right away, as per our planning. From this point, we will directly start PHP application development using NetBeans with a new PHP project, and make a good practice of the IDE. We know what to do, and within a few minutes we will learn how to do it.

Understanding JSON – JavaScript Object Notation

JavaScript Object Notation (JSON) is a lightweight, data-interchange format, and is easy for humans to read and write with. It is an easy format for machines to parse and generate, and is based on a subset of the JavaScript programming language. JSON is a text format that is completely language-independent.

JSON is built on two structures:

- ◆ A collection of name/value pairs: In various languages, this is realized as an object, record, struct, dictionary, hash table, keyed list, or an associative array.

- ◆ An ordered list of values: In most languages, this is realized as an array, vector, list, or sequence.

For example:

```
{ "firstName":"John" , "lastName":"Doe" }
```

Introducing jQuery – the definitive JavaScript library

jQuery is a fast and concise JavaScript library, which simplifies **DOM** (Document Object Model) traversing, event handling, animating, and AJAX interactions for rapid web development. jQuery is designed to change the way that you write JavaScript—http://jquery.com/.

Some of the reasons why we should use jQuery are as follows:

- ◆ Free and open source software
- ◆ Lightweight footprint
- ◆ CSS3-compliant
- ◆ Cross-browser
- ◆ Minimal code
- ◆ Off-the-shelf plugins

In simple terms, jQuery enables you to produce powerful and dynamic user interfaces.

 With the help of various jQuery plugins, including image slider, content slider, pop-up boxes, tabbed content, and so on, the developer's job might be minimized, because all they have to do is tweak or customize the small parts of the jQuery plugin into bigger parts, which they've used to match their demands.

Understanding AJAX – asynchronous JavaScript and XML

Asynchronous JavaScript and XML (AJAX) is a programming technique or approach used on the client-side to asynchronously retrieve the data from the server in the background, without interfering with the display and behavior of the existing page. Data is usually retrieved using the XMLHttpRequest object. Despite the name, the use of XML is not actually required, nor do the requests need to be asynchronous.

The jQuery library has a full suite of AJAX capabilities. The functions and methods therein allow us to load the data from the server without a browser page refresh.

Introducing jQuery.ajax()

Let's have a look at the sample jQuery.ajax() API.

```
$.ajax({
  url: "my_ajax_responder.php",
  type: "POST",

  data: {'name': 'Tonu'}, //key value paired or can be like
    "call=login&name=Tonu"

  success: function(xh){
    //success handler or callback
  },

  error: function(){
    //error handler
    }

});
```

In the $.ajax() function, you can see that the AJAX configuration object (created using the JavaScript object literal) is passed into it, and those configurations can be described as follows:

- url denotes the URL of the server script to communicate with
- type denotes the HTTP request type; that is GET/POST
- data contains the data to be sent to the server in the form of either a key value pair or as URL parameters
- success holds the AJAX success callback or method to perform on fetched data
- error holds the AJAX error callback

Now, let's have another example where `jQuery.ajax()` simply loads a JavaScript file from the server:

```
$.ajax({
    type: "GET",
    url: "test.js",
    dataType: "script"
});
```

Here, `dataType` defines the kind of data to be retrieved from the server; such a kind can be XML, JSON, `script`, plain text, and so on.

Introducing PHP Data Objects (PDO)

The **PHP Data Objects (PDO)** extension defines a lightweight and consistent interface for accessing databases in PHP. PDO provides a data-access abstraction layer, which means that regardless of which database you're using, you use the same functions to issue the queries and fetch the data. PDO does not provide database abstraction; it doesn't rewrite SQL or emulate missing features. You should use a full-blown abstraction layer if you need that facility.

It's worth mentioning that PDO supports prepared statements, which are:

- ◆ **Safer**: PDO or the underlying database library will take care of escaping the bound variables for you. You will never be vulnerable to SQL injection attacks if you always use prepared statements.

- ◆ **(Sometimes) Faster**: Many databases will cache the query plan for a prepared statement and refer to the prepared statement with a symbol, instead of retransmitting the entire query text. This is most noticeable if you prepare a statement only once, and then reuse the prepared statement object with different variables.

PHP 5.3 comes with a PDO and PDO_MYSQL driver built-in. More at `http://www.php.net/manual/en/book.pdo.php`.

Creating the NetBeans PHP project

After finishing planning the task, we are going the deal with its practical implementation.

Press *Ctrl+Shift+N* to start the new NetBeans PHP project and proceed with the creation of a new project as already discussed in *Chapter 1, Setting up your Development Environment*. Let's name the project as `chapter3` for our tutorial.

As we have created the PHP project, we will have the `index.php` file created automatically inside the project. So, the project can be located by pointing your browser to `http://localhost/chapter3/`.

Creating the status stream display list

According to the first part of our project, we will now create the status stream display list. In order to do this, we need a PHP class and a MySQL database, filled with some dummy data representing status posts. The PHP class, StatusPoster.php, will contain the MySQL database connection using the PDO inside its constructor, and a method to fetch the rows of status entries from the database.

Setting up the database server

To store and retrieve the status posts from the database, we connect with the MySQL database server, create the database and table to insert status entries, and fetch those entries to display within a status stream.

Time for action – connecting with MySQL database server

In this section, we will create a MySQL server connection by giving access credentials to the IDE, which displays a list of available databases under that connection in the IDE:

1. First of all, we will create the MySQL database server connection inside the IDE; press *Ctrl+5* to bring the **Services** window to focus, expand the **Databases** node, right-click on **MySQL Database Server**, and choose **Properties** to open the **MySQL Server Properties** window, as shown in the following screenshot:

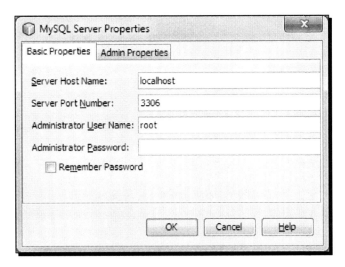

In the previous screenshot, the IDE already filled in the default values for the MySQL server details, such as the hostname, port number, username, and the password you just added. You may update these details at any time, as and when you need to.

2. Click on the **Admin Properties** tab, which allows you to enter the information for controlling your MySQL server. Click on the **OK** button to save the setting.

3. Now, you should have all the available databases listed under the **MySQL Server** node, as shown in the following screenshot:

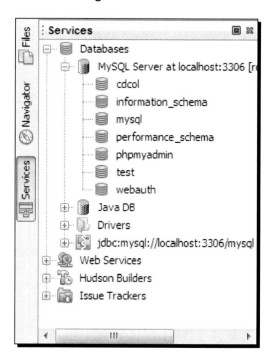

What just happened?

We have successfully connected with the MySQL server and listed all the databases available for the provided database user. We actually made the MySQL databases accessible from the IDE, so that we can directly operate any sort of database queries from the IDE in a quick way. Now, we will create a new database and table in there.

 See *Appendix* for NetBeans IDE keyboard shortcuts.

Creating the database and table

It's a common practice to have separate databases for each project. So, we will use a new database for our project, and a table to store entries. The IDE provides excellent GUI facilities for database management, such as SQL editor, query output viewer, and table viewer with column list.

Time for action – creating MySQL database and table

From the **MySQL Server** node, we shall create a new database and run a query to create the table along with the necessary column fields.

1. From the **Services** window, right-click on the **MySQL Server** node, and select **Create Database...**. A new dialog box will appear, as shown in the following screenshot:

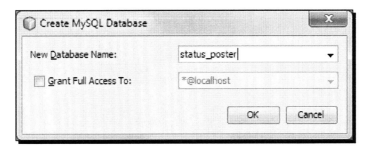

2. Enter the name `status_poster` as the value for the **New Database Name** field. Leave the checkbox for **Grant Full Access to** unselected. You may grant access to a given user, using this checkbox and drop-down list. By default, the `admin` user has all the permissions.

3. Click on **OK** to have the new database listed under the server node, and also to have the new database connection node created under the **Databases** node, as shown in the following screenshot:

According to this screenshot, there are three subfolders under the `status_poster` connection node—**Tables**, **Views**, and **Procedures**.

4. Now, to create a new table in our database, right-click on the **Tables** folder and choose **Execute Command...** to open the **SQL Editor** canvas in the main window, as follows:

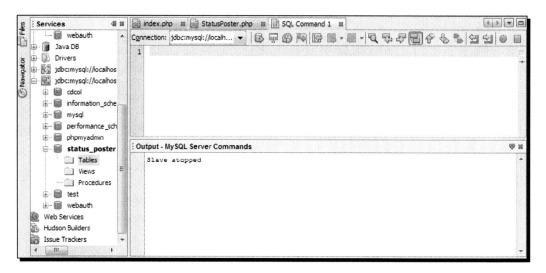

5. In the SQL editor, type the following query to create the new `Status` table:

```
CREATE TABLE `status` (
  `id` bigint(20) NOT NULL AUTO_INCREMENT,
  `name` varchar(50) NOT NULL,
  `image` varchar(100) NOT NULL,
  `status` varchar(500) NOT NULL,
  `timestamp` int(11) unsigned NOT NULL,
  PRIMARY KEY (`id`)
) ENGINE=MyISAM  DEFAULT CHARSET=utf8;
```

As you can see, we have `id` (auto incremented with each entry) as the primary key in the `status` table. We have the `name` field to store user names of up to `50` characters. The `image` field will store user thumbnail images of up to `100` characters. The `status` field will store user status posts of maximum `500` characters, and the `timestamp` field will keep a track of the time when the status was posted. The database engine has chosen `MyISAM` to provide faster table entries.

So, all you need to do is just type in the MySQL query inside the NetBeans query editor, and run the query to have your database ready.

6. To execute the query, either click on the **Run SQL** button in the task bar at the top (*Ctrl+Shift+E*), or right-click within the SQL editor and choose **Run Statement**. The IDE then generates the status table in the database, and you will receive a message similar to the following in the **Output** window:

```
Output - SQL Command 1 execution

  Executed successfully in 0.059 s, 0 rows affected.
  Line 1, column 1

  Execution finished after 0.059 s, 0 error(s) occurred.
```

7. You will also have your table status listed under the **Table** subfolder, under the `status_poster` database connection, as shown in the following screenshot:

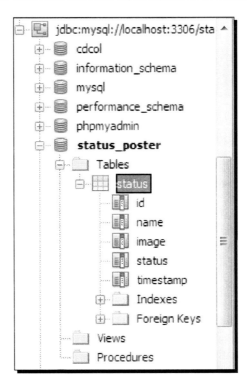

In this screenshot, the expanded status table shows the created columns with the primary key marked in red.

What just happened?

The IDE reveals the database management features; the creation of all those databases and tables can be done with a few clicks and keystrokes. Queries can be run within the IDE in a prompt manner, and the SQL command's execution output is displayed in a separate window. Next, we will insert a few sample entries into the created table to display them at the status stream list. We have to add some demo user-image files as well for this tutorial.

You can create a table by using the **Create Table** wizard, in **Database Explorer**—right-click on the **Tables** node and choose **Create Table**. The **Create Table** dialog box opens, from where you can add columns for the table with specific attributes.

See *Appendix* for NetBeans IDE keyboard shortcuts.

Inserting sample rows into the table

Right-click on the `status` table under the **Tables** subfolder, choose **Execute Command…**, and type the following query in the SQL editor, to insert some sample rows into the `status` table:

```
INSERT INTO `status` VALUES('', 'Rintu Raxan', 'rintu.jpg', 'On a day
in the year of fox', 1318064723);
INSERT INTO `status` VALUES('', 'Aminur Rahman', 'ami.jpg', 'Watching
inception first time', 1318064721);
INSERT INTO `status` VALUES('', 'Salim Uddin', 'salim.jpg', 'is very
busy with my new pet project smugBox', 1318064722);
INSERT INTO `status` VALUES('', 'M A Hossain Tonu', 'tonu.jpg', 'Hello
this is my AJAX posted status inserted by the StatusPoster PHP class',
1318067362);
```

You can see that we have a few MySQL `INSERT` queries to store some test users' data, such as name, image, status post, and Unix timestamp, for the status stream display list. Each such `INSERT` query inserts a row into the `status` table.

So, we have some sample rows in our table. In order to verify that the records have been added to the `status` table, right-click on the `status` table and choose **View Data...**. A new SQL editor tab opens in the main window with the `select * from status` query inside the SQL editor. Executing this statement will generate a tabular data viewer in the lower region of the main window, as shown in the following screenshot:

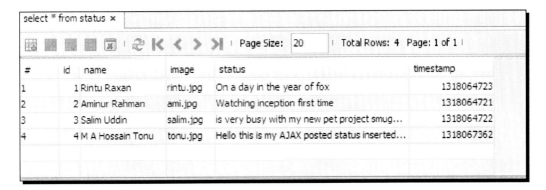

This SQL query is quite self-explanatory, where the `SELECT` keyword is used to select data from the table, and the SQL shorthand — `*` is used to denote that all the columns should be selected from the table.

Adding sample user image files

In this tutorial, we have inserted some sample rows to the `status` table; in the `image` column, we have some user image filenames, which we actually stored under the `user` folder, inside the project's `images` directory. Those sample user images can be found inside the project's source of this chapter. Download this complete project source from the Packt Publishing website and copy the sample user images.

To create a subfolder inside the `project` folder, right-click on the `chapter3` project node, and select **New | Folder...**; type the folder name `images` inside the **New Folder** dialog box, and click on **Finish** to create the folder. Now create another folder under the `images` directory named "`user`" in the same way, and put the copied sample user image files there.

Creating the StatusPoster PHP class

The purpose of the `StatusPoster` PHP class is to query the database for fetching and inserting status entries. A method of this class will be used to insert the status entries into that database table, and another method will be used to perform the action of fetching entries from the table. Simply, the class will serve as a database agent and can be used for necessary database operations.

Time for action – creating a class, adding a constructor, and creating methods

We will create the `StatusPoster.php` file and the class skeleton using the NetBeans code template, and to create methods within the class, we will use the `function` template as well. We will create a MySQL database connection using a PDO inside the class constructor, so that the database connection is created along with the object instantiation and `getStatusPosts()` method to fetch the status posts from the table.

1. From the **Projects** pane, right-click on project name `chapter3`, select **New | PHP File...**, and name the file `StatusPoster`, as shown in the following screenshot:

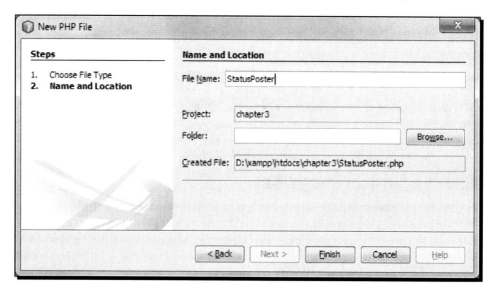

2. Click on **Finish** to have the file added to our project and automatically opened in the editor. You will see PHP starting and ending tags placed inside the file.

3. In order to create the PHP class skeleton, we will use PHP code templates. We type `cls` and press the *Tab* key to obtain the class skeleton with a constructor inside, as follows:

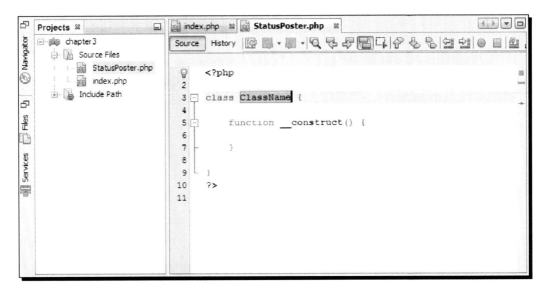

4. In the preceding screenshot, `classname` is already selected. You will just have to type `StatusPoster` as the value for `classname`, and press the *Tab key* to select the constructor name, as shown in the following screenshot:

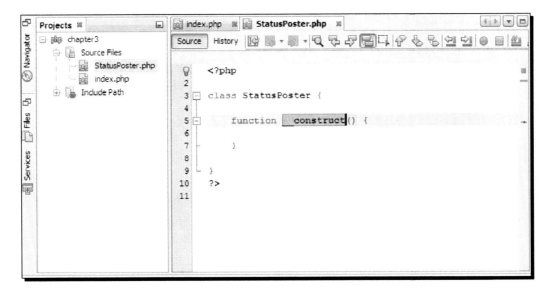

The constructor name remains intact, as it is the default PHP 5 naming convention for the constructor.

5. Now, add some class constants and attributes to hold the database credentials, as shown in the following code snippet:

```
class StatusPoster {
    private $db = NULL;

    const DB_SERVER = "localhost";
    const DB_USER = "root";
    const DB_PASSWORD = "root";
    const DB_NAME = "status_poster";

    public function __construct() {

    }

}
```

You can see the class constants added, which contain database information, such as the database server name, username, password, and database name, respectively. A `private` class variable `$db` has been added to hold the database connection inside a PDO object. You may modify those constants as per your own requirements.

> **Private**: This property or method can be used only by the class or object that it is a part of; it cannot be accessed elsewhere.

6. To fetch the status posts from the `status` table, we will add an empty method named `getStatusPosts` inside the class. To do this, type `fnc` and press *Tab* to have the empty function code generated with the selected function name. Type the selected function name as `getStatusPosts`, and drop the parameter `$param` variable this time. Our class skeleton will look similar to the following:

```
class StatusPoster {
    private $db = NULL;

    const DB_SERVER = "localhost";
    const DB_USER = "root";
    const DB_PASSWORD = "root";
    const DB_NAME = "status_poster";
```

```
    public function __construct() {

    }
    public function getStatusPosts() {

    }
}
```

We have our class skeleton ready, and we shall add code inside those class methods. Now, we will create the database connection code inside the constructor.

7. To connect MySQL using PDO, type the following lines inside the class constructor so that it looks similar to the following code snippet:

```
public function __construct() {
    $dsn = 'mysql:dbname='.self::DB_NAME.';host='.self::DB_SERVER;

    try {
        $this->db = new PDO($dsn, self::DB_USER, self::DB_
PASSWORD);
    } catch (PDOException $e) {
        throw new Exception('Connection failed: ' .
        $e->getMessage());
    }

    return $this->db;
}
```

`public function __construct ()` connects with the MySQL database using a PDO—the database connection in terms of a PDO instance is stored in the class's `private` variable.

The `$dsn` variable contains **Data Source Name (DSN)**, which holds the information required to connect to the database. One of the biggest advantages of using PDO is that if we want to migrate to other SQL solutions, then all we need to do is adjust the DSN parameter string.

The following line creates a PDO instance to represent a connection to the requested database, and returns a PDO object on success:

```
$this->db = new PDO($dsn, self::DB_USER, self::DB_PASSWORD);
```

Note that it throws a `PDOException` exception if the attempt to connect to the requested database fails.

8. To select the status posts from the table, we shall write a `select` query with the help of an auto completion code inside the `getStatusPosts` method. As we discussed in the previous chapter, SQL code completion begins with the SQL keyword `SELECT` and by pressing *Ctrl+Space bar*. So, we will proceed according to these steps and write the following query code inside this method:

```
public function getStatusPosts() {

    $statement = $this->db->prepare("SELECT name, image, status,
timestamp FROM status ORDER BY timestamp DESC,id");
    $statement->execute();

        if ($statement->rowCount() > 0) {
            return $statement->fetchAll();
        }

        return false;
}
```

With this code, we selected columns (`name`, `image`, `status`, and `timestamp`), from the table status ordered by timestamp, in descending order. We also selected `id` in ascending order, by default. The `prepare()` method prepares the SQL statement to be executed by the `PDOStatement::execute()` method. After the `execute()` method, if rows are found, then it fetches and returns all the table entries.

9. Now, we will instantiate an object of this class at the bottom of this file, with the following line:

```
$status = new StatusPoster();
```

What just happened?

The PDO instance is created at the class constructor and is stored in the `$db` variable, so other member methods can access this class variable as `$this->db`, to use PDO methods such as `prepare()`, `execute()`.

Calling `PDO::prepare()` and `PDOStatement::execute()` for statements that will be issued multiple times optimizes the performance, by caching of the query plan and meta information, and so on.

Up to now, we have our database operations code ready inside `StatusPoster.php`. We will create an HTML user interface to display the status list fetched from the database table status.

 See *Appendix* for NetBeans IDE keyboard shortcuts.

1. Which one is not a PDO feature?

    a. Prepared statements

    b. Bind value

    c. Bind object

    d. Data access abstraction

Firing the user interface for displaying the status list

The HTML user interface will display the status list retrieved by the `getStatusPosts` method from the `StatusPoster` class, and the user will be able to view the list of status posts from his test friends along with his own posts. The interface will use jQuery and the status list styled by the CSS classes.

Time for action – adding CSS support to the document

We shall use `index.php` as our single page interface for the application, and will add the CSS stylesheet support to the document. To maintain practice, we will try to put style attributes into classes, so that they become reusable and can be utilized as an element's class name whenever a specific class of styles is required. So, let's create the CSS classes first:

1. Create a folder named `styles` inside our project source directory for our CSS file.

2. To create a **Cascading Style Sheet** where CSS classes reside, right-click on the `styles` folder inside the project, select **New | Cascading Style Sheet** from the **New Cascading Style Sheet** dialog box, name the CSS file as `styles.css`, and hit **Finish**. Drop all the comments and code blocks in the opened CSS file. Type the following style classes in the CSS file:

```
body {
    font-family:Arial,Helvetica,sans-serif;
    font-size:12px;
}

h1,input {
    color:#fff;
    background-color:#1A3C6C;
}

h1,input,textarea,.inputbox,.postStatus {
    padding:5px;
```

```css
}

input,textarea,ul li img,.inputbox {
    border:1px solid #ccc;
}

ul li {
    width:100%;
    display:block;
    border-bottom:1px solid #ccc;
    padding:10px 0;
}

ul li img {
    padding:2px;
}

.container {
    width:60%;
    float:none;
    margin:auto;
}

.content {
    padding-left:15px;
}

.content a {
    font-weight:700;
    color:#3B5998;
    text-decoration:none;
}

.clearer {
    clear:both;
}

.hidden {
    display:none;
}

.left {
    float:left;
```

```
}

.right {
    float:right;
}

.localtime {
    color:#999;
}

.inputbox {
    height:70px;
    margin:15px 0;
}

.inputbox textarea {
    width:450px;
    height:50px;
    overflow:hidden;
}

.inputbox input {
    margin-right:30px;
    width:50px;
}
```

We will use a `container` class to apply styles on the application interface container `<div>` inside the document body; `ul li` will represent the listed items, which are status `li` items with the parent `ul` element, and other HTML elements, such as `h1`, `img`, and `textarea`, which are also styled using CSS classes.

3. Add the following PHP code snippet at the top of the `index.php` file:

```php
<?php
define('BASE_URL', 'http://localhost/chapter3/');
?>
```

We have defined a PHP constant for defining the base URL for the web application. The base URL can be used to provide an absolute path for the project asset files (CSS or JS files). You may put your project directory name in place of `chapter3`.

4. Now, add the following line to your `index.php` document heading below the `<title>` tag, to include the CSS file.

```
<link href="<?=BASE_URL?>styles/styles.css" media="screen"
rel="stylesheet"
   type="text/css" />
```

With this line, we have embedded the CSS file into our HTML document. Here, `BASE_URL` tells us that the file `styles/styles.css` is available under the project directory. So, our interface elements will inherit styles from the `styles.css` file.

What just happened?

In order to maintain a consistent interface over browsers, various HTML elements have been styled using the CSS classes, and some classes are written from where the assignee elements will inherit the styles.

In order to maintain the CSS code to minimum lines, comma separated classes or element names have been used for sharing common attributes, as follows:

```
h1, input, textarea, .inputbox, .postStatus{
    padding:5px;
}
```

Here, the `padding:5px;` style will be applied to the mentioned elements or with the given classes. Therefore, common attributes among the classes can be mitigated in this way.

To understand the class reusability issue, let's have a look at the following:

```
.left {
    float:left;
}
```

We can use `left` as the class name for multiple elements, which need the `float:left` style, such as `<div class="left">`, `<img class="left" />`, and so on.

Time for action – adding jQuery support and custom JS library

We will add a jQuery (a JavaScript library; more at `http://jquery.com/`) support to the document and create a jQuery-based, custom JS library.

For the JS library, we will create a separate JavaScript file, `status.js`, where the interface JS code will reside to serve interface tasks, such as posting statuses via AJAX and some utility methods for displaying the local date-time. So, let's create our custom JS library:

1. To add the jQuery support from Google Content Delivery Network (CDN) to our document, add the following lines to your `index.php` document heading below the `<link>` tag:

```
<script src=
  "http://ajax.googleapis.com/ajax/libs/jquery/1.7/jquery.min.js">
</script>
```

With this line, we have the latest jQuery version from the CDN. Note that version 1.7 means the latest available version, which is 1.7.X, unless you have specified the exact number, which is 1.7.2 or greater. Now, our document is jQuery-enabled and ready to use the jQuery features.

2. To create the jQuery-based custom JS library, add a new JavaScript file inside the `js` folder, and name it as `status.js`. Include the file in your document head, so that the `<head>` tag looks similar to the following code snippet:

```
<head>
    <meta http-equiv="Content-Type" content="text/html;
charset=UTF-8">
    <title>Status updater</title>
    <link href="<?=BASE_URL?>styles/styles.css" media="screen"
rel="stylesheet" type="text/css" />
    <script src="http://ajax.googleapis.com/ajax/libs/jquery/1.7/
jquery.min.js"></script>
    <script src="<?=BASE_URL?>js/status.js"></script>
  </head>
```

3. Now, create the `Status` JS library skeleton inside the `status.js` file, as follows:

```
$(document).ready(function ($)
{

var Status = {

};

});
```

You can see that the variable `Status` contains an object using the JavaScript object literal (key value pairs enclosed within curly braces).

```
var obj = { a : function(){ }, b : function(){ } }
```

Note that the library code is wrapped with the jQuery `$(document).ready()` function.

4. Let's write some utility JavaScript methods inside the `status` object and type the following `currentTime ()` method:

```
currentTime: function (timestamp) {

    if (typeof timestamp !== 'undefined' && timestamp !== '')
        var currentTime = new Date(timestamp * 1000);
    else
        var currentTime = new Date();

    var hours = currentTime.getHours();
    var minutes = currentTime.getMinutes();
    var timeStr = '';
    if (minutes < 10) {
        minutes = "0" + minutes
    }
    timeStr = ((hours > 12) ? (hours - 12) : hours) + ":" +
minutes + ' ';
    if (hours > 11) {
        timeStr += "PM";
    } else {
        timeStr += "AM";
    }
    return timeStr;
},
```

The `currentTime ()` method returns the local time converted from the Unix timestamp. Remember that if the timestamp is not present, then it returns the current local time. A sample output could be 3:22 AM or 2:30 PM.

You can see that in the line `var currentTime = new Date(timestamp * 1000);`, the Unix timestamp has been converted to the JS timestamp in milliseconds, and a new `Date` object has been created. Hours and minutes are picked from the `currentTime.getHours()` and `currentTime. getMinutes ()` methods, respectively. Note that the `currentTime ()` method is delimited with a comma (,).

5. Add the `currentDate ()` method inside the `Status` object, as follows:

```
currentDate: function (timestamp) {
    var m_names = ["January", "February", "March", "April", "May",
"June", "July", "August", "September", "October", "November",
"December"];

    if (typeof timestamp !== 'undefined' && timestamp !== '')
        var d = new Date(timestamp * 1000);
    else
        var d = new Date();


    var curr_date = d.getDate();
    var curr_month = d.getMonth();
    var curr_year = d.getFullYear();
    var sup = "";
    if (curr_date === 1 || curr_date === 21 || curr_date === 31)
    {
        sup = "st";
    }
    else if (curr_date === 2 || curr_date === 22)
    {
        sup = "nd";
    }
    else if (curr_date === 3 || curr_date === 23)
    {
        sup = "rd";
    }
    else
    {
        sup = "th";
    }

    return m_names[curr_month] + ' ' + curr_date + sup + ', ' +
curr_year;

},
```

The `currentDate ()` method returns the converted local date. Similar to the previous method in *step 4*, it fetches the date, month, and year from the `Date` object.

6. Now, add the `getLocalTimeStr ()` method as follows:

```
getLocalTimeStr: function (gmtTimestampInSec) {
    return 'at ' + this.currentTime(gmtTimestampInSec)
        + ' on ' + this.currentDate(gmtTimestampInSec);
}
```

The above method returns the formatted time and date concatenated in a string.

What just happened?

jQuery provides us with a special utility on the document object called `ready`, allowing us to execute the code only after the DOM has completely finished loading. Using `$(document).ready()`, we can queue up a series of events and have them executed after the DOM is initialized. The `$(document).ready()` method takes a function (anonymous) as its argument, which is passed to be called after the DOM has finished loading, and executes the code inside the function.

If you are developing code for distribution, it's always important to compensate for any possible name clashing. So we passed `$` as an argument for the anonymous function. That `$` refers to `jQuery` inside, and hence the other `$` functions, which are imported after the script, don't conflict.

Finally, to obtain the local date and time from the UNIX timestamp, we have added the utility methods in our custom JavaScript library. As for a usage example, the `currentDate()` utility method can be called as `this.currentDate()` and `Status.currentDate()` from the object's inside and outside scope, respectively.

Time for action – showing the status list

We shall put the interface elements inside `index.php`, and embed the PHP code in an appropriate way. So, let's go through the steps:

1. Modify the `index.php` file inside the `<body>` tag, drop the PHP tag, and place the status entries in the `<div>` container tag and elements, as follows:

```
<body>
  <div id="container" class="container">

    <h1>Status Poster</h1>

    <ul>

    </ul>

  </div>
</body>
```

From this code, you can see that our application interface will be within the `<div>` container with the id container, and the `<ul>` tag will hold the inner `<li>` items' stack containing the status posts from the users, which will be populated by some PHP codes.

2. Above the `<!DOCTYPE html>` tag, at the top PHP code snippet of the `index.php` file, type the following lines to integrate the `StatusPoster` class so that the code snippet looks similar to the following:

```php
<?php
require_once 'StatusPoster.php';

$result = $status->getStatusPosts();
define('BASE_URL', 'http://localhost/chapter3/');
?>
```

From the code, the PHP class file is required once to integrate the class, and use its instance into our application. At this line, we called the `getStatusPosts()` method of the `$status` object to get all the status entries from the database, and the returned resultant array is stored into `$result` as well.

3. To display a status stream, we will write the following PHP code to loop through the `$result` array inside the `<ul>` tag:

```php
<?php
if (is_array($result))
foreach ($result as $row) {
    echo '
        <li>
            <a href="#">
                <img class="left" src="images/user/' .
$row['image'] . '" alt="picture">
            </a>
            <div class="content left">
                <a href="#">' . $row['name'] . '</a>
                <div class="status">' . $row['status'] . '</div>
                <span class="localtime" data-timestamp="' .
$row['timestamp'] . '"></span>
            </div>
            <div class="clearer"></div>
        </li>
        ';
}
?>
```

At first, the `$result` array has been verified for its proper type. We looped through the array to have each entry into the `$row` variable. The preceding server script generates one `<li>` item for each status entry, and each `<li>` item contains a user image, a hyperlinked name, a user status text, and a UNIX timestamp element. Note that the timestamp has been dumped into the `data-timestamp` attribute of a span element with the class name `localtime`. For a better understanding, an item skeleton of the status list is shown in the following diagram:

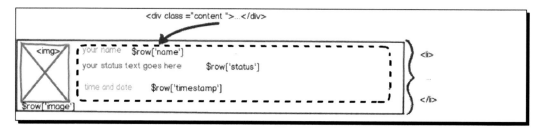

4. Now, we need to convert the PHP-dumped timestamp inside the `data-timestamp` attribute using the jQuery code, as soon as the DOM is ready. Add the following method inside the `Status` object of the library `status.js`:

```
showLocalTime: function () {
    var spans = $('span.localtime[data-timestamp]');

    spans.each( function () {
        var localTimeStr  = Status.getLocalTimeStr( $(this).
attr('data-timestamp') );
        $(this).html(localTimeStr);
    });
},
```

The method, using jQuery selector, selects all the span elements having the data-timestamp attribute with `$('span.localtime[data-timestamp]');`. For each element, it parses the timestamp with `$(this).attr('data-timestamp')`, and passes to `Status.getLocalTimeStr()` to obtain the local time string. Finally, it sets the inner HTML of each span element with that local time string.

5. To enable `Status.showLocalTime()` to work immediately with DOM, call the method, as follows, before the termination line of `ready()` method:

```
$(document).ready(function ($)
{
var Status = {
    //whole library methods...
};

Status.showLocalTime();
});
```

So, the users will be displayed with their local date and time under each post.

6. Finally, point your browser with the project URL, or press the **Run Project (chapter3)** button from the toolbar, or press *F6* from the IDE to have the status stream display the list, which looks similar to the following screenshot:

What just happened?

The PHP script dumps the `<li>` items inside the `<ul>` tag, and the interface JS code `Status.showLocalTime();` parses the dumped timestamp and displays it in the user's local time, as soon as the DOM is ready. In case we display the date and time from the UNIX timestamp without the time zone conversion, then we may have to deliver the server's date and time, which may not conform to the user's time. Again, the user's local timezone is unknown to the server and known to the client interface. So in a quick way, we used a client-end code to solve the local time display issue.

Hence, we've completed the first part of our project. We have created the interface where the status stream looks like Facebook.

Until now, we have been able to deal with the database operation using the IDE, and with the PHP class and method creation using the NetBeans code template, we have also been able to create the necessary user interface files for our web application.

Have a go hero – tweaking the CSS

For large status posts, the interface can be found broken inside each `<li>`, so it would be best to fix the user interface issue. You may add fixed width into the `.content` class in the corresponding CSS file.

Pop quiz – understanding CSS

1. What does CSS stand for?

    a. Cascaded Style Sheet

    b. Cascading Style Sheet

    c. Colorful Style Sheet

    d. Computer Style Sheet

2. What is the correct HTML format for referring to an external stylesheet?

    a. `<link rel="stylesheet" type="text/css" href="mystyle.css">`

    b. `<style src="mystyle.css">`

    c. `<stylesheet>mystyle.css</stylesheet>`

3. What property needs to be added into the CSS class to have some space around that element?

    a. `padding`

    b. `margin`

    c. `padding-bottom and padding-top`

    d. `display`

Hatching out the status poster using PHP-AJAX

The user's status text should be submitted to the server without reloading the page. To do this we can use the AJAX approach, where the user's data can be sent to the server with the HTTP methods, and wait for the server's response. As soon as the server responds, we can parse the response data and may take our decision programmatically. In our case, if the server responded with a success result, we will update our interface DOM according to that.

Simply, we will use AJAX to submit the user's status text with the HTTP POST method to our server-side PHP code residing at index.php, and we will configure the expected data type from the server to be JSON. So, we can easily parse the JSON and determine whether the status was saved successfully or not. From a successful server response, we can update the status stream display list and place the newly posted status at the top of that list. However, in the case of any failure or error, we can parse the error message and display that into the interface as well.

Time for action – adding the status input box to the interface

In this section, we will simply add an HTML form consisting of one text area for the status post and a **Submit** button for the form submission. We will add the form wrapped with a div element before the `<ul>` tag at index.php.

1. In order to add the status poster box, we add the following HTML code inside the div#container, **before the** `<ul>` tag:

```
<div class="inputbox">
<form id="statusFrom" action="index.php" method="post" >
    <textarea name="status" id="status_box">Write your status
here</textarea>
    <input class="right" type="submit" name="submit" id="submit"
value="Share" />
    <div id="postStatus" class="postStatus clearer
hidden">loading</div>
</form>
</div>
```

So, the div.inputbox will contain the status input box with a share or submit button. div#postStatus will display the post submission progress information status that conveys it, whether the status was successfully posted or not. We will use some fancy loading .gif image while the AJAX post is in progress. The ajaxload. gif image is also kept inside the project's images directory.

2. Now, refresh your browser with the project URL, and the status input box should look similar to the following screenshot:

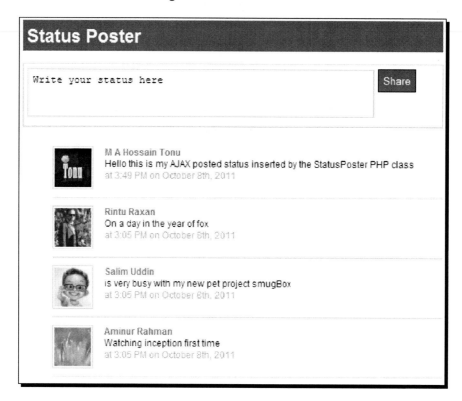

What just happened?

Check out the line where the `form` tag opened, `<form id="statusFrom" action="index.php" method="post" >`. The form can be selected with the `id` attribute using the jQuery `action` attribute that contains the script name as `index.php`, which means that it will be posted to the same file we are working on. You can see that the `method` attribute contains the HTTP method type in which the form will be submitted. We don't need the `action` and `method` attributes for the jQuery code. Rather, we will keep them in this case. If the browser's JavaScript is disabled, then we could still submit the form to `index.php` in the `POST` method.

Note that `div#postStatus` is hidden by default using the CSS class `hidden`, and will be visible only while AJAX works in progress.

 See *Appendix* for the NetBeans IDE keyboard shortcuts.

Adding new status post template to index.php

We need to maintain a separation of behavior while coding, as HTML markups shall be kept separate from JavaScript codes. Also, we need to update the status stream display list, and put the new status post at the top of the list without page reloading.

We know that each status entry can be organized inside an `<li>` item, where inside that item, the entry values such as username, image, and status post with local date-time mentioned beneath, should be crafted with appropriate markup elements. So, we need to create an entry template for the new status post. Using the template, JavaScript code can generate a new interface entry to be placed on top of the status stream.

Add the following template inside the document `<body>` tag, below the `div#container` ending tag:

```
<div id="statusTemplate" class="hidden">
<li>
    <a href="#">
        <img class="left" src="#SRC" alt="picture">
    </a>
    <div class="content left">
        <a href="#">#NAME</a>
        <div class="status">#STATUS</div>
        <span class="localtime">#TIME</span>
    </div>
    <div class="clearer"></div>
</li>
</div>
```

We can see that there are placeholders, such as `#SRC` for the profile picture's image URL, `#NAME` for name of the user for the entry, `#STATUS` for status text, and `#TIME` for local date-time. By making a copy of this template, these placeholders can be replaced with appropriate values and prepended at the `<ul>` element. Note that the entire template is kept inside a hidden `div` element to exclude it from the user's view.

Creating the AJAX status poster

AJAX is used to communicate frequently from a browser to the web server. Such a famous technique is being vastly used in **Rich Internet Applications (RIA)**, and jQuery provides a very simple AJAX framework. The AJAX poster will post the status texts without page reloading, and will update the status stack with the latest status entry at the top.

Time for action – creating status poster using JQuery AJAX

We will create a post() method inside the status.js library, and bind the method with the click event on the **Submit** button. We will create the method by adding code lines one after another, as shown in the following steps:

1. At our status.js library, type the following post() method, terminated with a comma, to add it inside the Status library:

```
post: function () {
    var myname = 'M A Hossain Tonu', myimage = 'images/user/tonu.
jpg';
    var loadingHtml = '<img src="images/ajaxload.gif"
alt="loadin.."  border="0" >';
    var successMsg = 'Status Posted Successfully ...';
    var statusTxt = $('#status_box').val(), postStatus =
$('#postStatus');

},
```

At the variable declaration section, the myname and myimage variables contain a demo logged-in, user's name and profile picture URL. The loadingHtml contains the img tag for displaying the loading GIF animation. Also, you can see that statusTxt contains the status box value obtained using $('#status_box'). val(), and postStatus caches the div#postStatus element.

2. Now, add the following line after the variables declaration section within the post() method:

```
if ((statusTxt.trim() !== '' && statusTxt !== 'Write your status
here'

    && statusTxt.length < 500) === false) return;
```

This code validates statusTxt if it is empty or if it contains a default input message, and even if it is within the maximum input limit of 500 characters. The method is returned after the execution, if any such validation fails.

3. To display animation loading while the AJAX operation is in progress, we can add the following line after the previous line (*step 2*):

```
postStatus.html(loadingHtml).fadeIn('slow');
```

It fades in #postStatus of the div element with the loading image inside.

4. Now, it's time to add the AJAX feature inside the method. Add the following jQuery code after the previous line (*step 3*):

```
$.ajax({
    data: $('form').serialize(),
    url: 'index.php',
    type: 'POST',
    dataType: 'json',
    success: function (response) {

        //ajax success callback codes
    },
    error: function () {}
});
```

In this code, you can see that the AJAX skeleton is added, and the jQuery `$.ajax()` method passed with configuration object. The configuration object is created using the JavaScript object literal technique. You can see those key-value pairs; for example, `data` contains the serialized values of the form using `$('form').serialize()`, `url` holds the server URL where the data is to be submitted, `dataType` is given as JSON so that we will have a JSON object passed inside the `success()` callback method. Check out the default `success` and `error` callback methods; you can see a variable `response` passed into the `success` callback, which is actually a JSON object fetched from the server using AJAX.

5. On successful AJAX submission, let's type the following code inside the `success` callback method:

```
if (response.success === true) {

    postStatus.html('<strong>'+successMsg+'</strong>');

    $('#status_box').val('');

    var statusHtml = $('#statusTemplate').html();
    statusHtml = statusHtml
                    .replace('#SRC', myimage)
                    .replace('#NAME', myname)
                    .replace('#STATUS', statusTxt)
                    .replace('#TIME', Status.getLocalTimeStr());

    $('#container ul').prepend(statusHtml);

} else {
    postStatus.html('<strong>' + response.error + '</strong>').
fadeIn("slow");
}
```

As `response` passed-in is a JSON object, we examine the `response` object for the `response.success` attribute, which contains Boolean `true` or `false` values. If the `response.success` attribute is not set to `true`, then display the error message from `response.error` inside the element `div#postStatus`.

So, for a success response from the server, we display the message inside `successMsg` and clear the input `text_area#status_box` value for the next input. Now, in the line `var statusHtml = $('#statusTemplate').html();`, we cached the entry template inside the `statusHtml` variable. At the consecutive lines, we have replaced the placeholders with proper entry values, and finally prepended the new entry item in the `<ul>` element, using the line `$('#container ul').prepend(statusHtml)`.

6. In order to trigger `Status.post()` with the event, we bind the method with the *click* event on the `Submit` (**share**) button. Add the following code inside `status.js` library before the termination of the `$(document).ready()` method (after `Status.showLocalTime()` line):

```
$('#submit').click(function () {
    Status.post();
    return false;
});
```

What just happened?

We have serialized the form values to be sent to the server via AJAX, and the server response was parsed by the jQuery AJAX feature to obtain a JSON object inside the `success` callback method. We examined whether the `response` object carries the `success` flag or not. In case a success flag was found, we used it to parse the status entry template to prepare the entry HTMLs and prepend the entry at the top of the status list.

So, we have the AJAX status poster method `post()` bound with the status **Submit** button, which fires with a click on the button. Note that we reflect the `success` or `error` messages at the user interface while the `post()` method executes, and even displays the loading animation. Hence, we made our application responsive.

Now, let's add the server code to respond to the AJAX request.

Working with StatusPoster.php again

To insert an entry into the database table's status field, we add a StatusPoster method to our PHP class, named insertStatus as follows:

```
public function insertStatus(array $values){

    $sql = "INSERT INTO status ";
    $fields = array_keys($values);
    $vals = array_values($values);

    $sql .= '('.implode(',', $fields).') ';

    $arr = array();
    foreach ($fields as $f) {
        $arr[] = '?';
    }
    $sql .= 'VALUES ('.implode(',', $arr).') ';

    $statement = $this->db->prepare($sql);

    foreach ($vals as $i=>$v) {
        $statement->bindValue($i+1, $v);
    }

    return $statement->execute();
}
```

The method takes the field values passed in an associative array, $values, prepares the MySQL insert query for the status table, and executes the query. Note that we have kept the field names in the $fields array and the field values in the $vals array extracted from the keys and values of the passed arrays. We have used ? in place of all the given values for the prepared statement, each of which will be replaced with corresponding values bound with the PDOStatement::bindValue() method. The bindValue() method binds a value to a parameter.

Note that variables containing direct user input should be escaped in order to make this data safe before sending in a query to MySQL. A PDO-prepared statement takes care of the escaping bound values for you.

Finally, the method returns, irrespective of whether the execute() method was successful or not.

Adding AJAX responder code to index.php

Add the following AJAX responder code inside the PHP code located at the top of the
index.php file, below the line `require_once 'StatusPoster.php';`:

```
if (isset($_POST['status'])) {
    $statusStr = trim($_POST['status']);
    $length = mb_strlen($statusStr);
    $success = false;

    if ($length > 0 && $length < 500) {
        $success = $status->insertStatus(array(
                'name' => 'M A Hossain Tonu',
                'image' => 'tonu.jpg',
                'status' => $statusStr,
                'timestamp' => time()
                ));
    }

    if (isset($_SERVER['HTTP_X_REQUESTED_WITH']) && $_SERVER['HTTP_X_
REQUESTED_WITH'] === 'XMLHttpRequest') {
        echo ($success) ? '{"success":true}' : '{"error":"Error
posting status"}';
        exit;
    }
}
```

This code checks if there is any POST value contained by $_POST['status']; if yes,
it trims the posted status value, and determines the length of the posted status string
contained in $statusStr. The length is measured using the multi-byte, string length
function mb_strlen(). If the string length is within the mentioned range, compact the
status entry values with the associated database column names within an array, and pass
the insertStatus method of the StatusPoster class to save the status.

As the insertStatus method returns true for successful database insertion, we kept the
returned value into the $success variable. Also, an AJAX request can be identified at server
by verifying the $_SERVER['HTTP_X_REQUESTED_WITH'] value is XMLHttpRequest.

So, for an AJAX request, we will deliver the JSON string; {"success":true} for $success
contains Boolean true, or {"error":"Error posting status"} for $success
contains Boolean false.

Therefore, checking for the value XMLHttpRequest ensures the JSON string delivery only
for the AJAX request. Finally, the preceding PHP code inserts the status post with or without
the AJAX request. So, in the case where JavaScript is disabled in the client browser, the status
poster form can still be submitted and the submitted data could be inserted as well.

The complete project source for this chapter can be downloaded from the Packt website URL.

Testing the usability of the status poster

We have the status poster project ready. The interface JavaScript code posts to the server, the server-side code performs the instructed actions and response, and the interface code updates the DOM along with the response.

You can test the status poster by typing in the box with your status texts, and clicking on the **Share** button. With the **Share** button-click, you should see a loading image below the input box. Within a few moments, you will see a **Status posted successfully** message, as the status gets prepended at the status display list. Finally, immediately after a status "**hello world**" has been posted, the screen looks similar to the following:

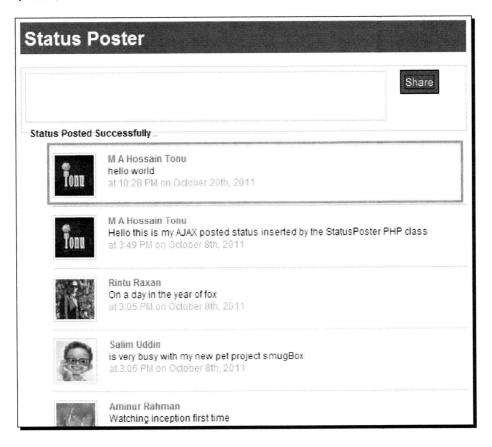

The completed project directory structure looks similar to the following:

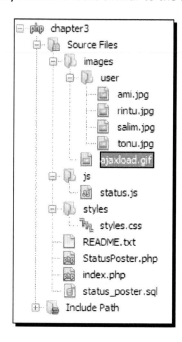

Pop quiz – Reviewing jQuery knowledge

1. Which sign does jQuery use as a shortcut for jQuery?

   a. The ? Sign

   b. The % sign

   c. The $ sign

   d. The jQuery sign

2. Which of the following is correct, to get the value of an input box using the `#element_id` ID?

   a. `$('#element_id').value()`

   b. `$('#element_id').text()`

   c. `$('#element_id').html()`

   d. `$('#element_id').val()`

3. Which of the following returns the length of a string stored inside the `stringVar` variable in JavaScript?

   a. `stringVar.size`

   b. `length(stringVar)`

   c. `stringVar.length`

4. What will be the correct statement to add a `DIV` element, inside at the beginning of another element?

   a. `$('#container').append('<div></div>');`

   b. `$('#container').html('<div></div>');`

   c. `$('#container').prepend('<div></div>');`

5. Which one of the following will cause an element to disappear gradually?

   a. `$('#element').hide();`

   b. `$('#element').fadeOut('slow');`

   c. `$('#element').blur('slow');`

6. Which one of the following will be the correct code to obtain the inner HTML of `element1` to use as inner HTML of `element2`?

   a. `$('#element2').html( ) = $('#element1').html( );`

   b. `$('#element2').html( $('#element1').innerHTML );`

   c. `$('#element1').html( $('#element2').html() );`

   d. `$('#element2').html( $('#element1').html( ) );`

Have a go hero – sanitizing the status input

Since the status input provided by the user is not sanitized enough, there are chances that raw markups or HTML tags placed inside the input will break the interface. So, sanitize the status input properly, and also take care of the JavaScript code that displays this new status entry without refreshing the page on success of AJAX. You may strip tags using the `trip_tags()` method from the input before inserting it into the `INSERT` query, if you wish not to allow tags. Again you may use the PHP `htmlspecialchars()` function if you wish to keep the tags. You have to refactor your JS codes as well; that is, you may use `$('#status_box').text()` instead of `$('#status_box').val()`.

Summary

In this chapter, we have done a real-life PHP project, and we are now able to create and maintain a PHP project using the NetBeans IDE. Also, we are now familiar with the usage of the IDE for faster development. Practicing those keyboard shortcuts, code completion short codes, code generators, and other IDE features will quicken your pace and smoothen your development. All these features are meant to simplify your tasks and make your life easier.

We have specially worked on:

- Setting up the database
- Creating the JavaScript library
- Real-life, PHP–AJAX, web application development
- Using NetBeans code templates

So far, we have developed a PHP project using NetBeans. In the next chapter, we will perform debugging and testing on some demo PHP projects to have more skills in dealing with critical moments in a project.

Debugging and Testing using NetBeans

If debugging is defined as the art of taking bugs out of a program, then programming must be putting them in.

In this chapter, we are going to learn to debug and test PHP web applications using NetBeans IDE. We will deal with sample projects, to learn the process of bug hunting and testing. The following topics will be discussed in this chapter:

◆ Configuring XDebug

◆ Debugging the PHP source code with XDebug

◆ Unit testing with PHPUnit and Selenium

◆ Code coverage

Let's go bug the hunter and do some real tricks...

Debugging – the ancient art of programming

After writing a program, the next step is to test the program to find whether it is working as desired or not. Sometimes, when we run our code for the first time just after it has been written, it may produce errors, such as syntax errors, runtime errors, and logical errors. Debugging is the step-by-step process of finding errors, so that the errors can be fixed to make the program work in the way it was intended.

Modern editors can detect almost all syntax errors, and hence we can fix them while typing code. Also, there are tools that can be integrated with the IDE to find bugs, and they are known as debuggers. There are a number of good debuggers, such as XDebug and FirePHP (for FireBug fans), for PHP. Such debuggers come with an application profiler as well. In this chapter, we'll try XDebug for debugging PHP projects using NetBeans.

Debugging PHP source code with XDebug

XDebug is highly configurable and adaptable to a variety of situations. You can inspect local variables, set watches, set breakpoints, and evaluate code, live. You can also navigate to declarations, types, and files using the **Go To** shortcuts and hypertext links. Use a global PHP `include` path for all projects or customize it per project.

The NetBeans IDE for PHP also offers command-line debugging. The PHP program output appears in a command-line display in the IDE itself, and you can inspect the generated HTML without having to switch to a browser.

You can debug scripts and web pages either locally or remotely. The NetBeans PHP debugger integration allows you to map server paths to local paths, in order to enable remote debugging.

XDebug offers features such as the following:

- ◆ Automatic stack tracing upon an error
- ◆ Function call logging
- ◆ Enhancing the `var_dump()` output and code-coverage information

Stack traces show you where errors occur, allowing you to trace function calls and the originating line numbers. The `var_dump()` output is displayed in a more elaborate way with XDebug.

> XDebug overrides PHP's default `var_dump()` function for displaying variable dumps. XDebug's version comprises different colors for different variable types, and places limits on the amount of array elements/object properties, maximum depth, and string lengths.

Configuring XDebug

Configuring XDebug is pretty much easy on each separate operating system. In this section, let's configure XDebug with our development environment, which is XAMPP, LAMP, and MAMP. All you have to do is enable some lines at `php.ini` or press some commands. As we have already installed the development pack, we will just activate XDebug on those stacks. First of all, we will get the tool working on our localhost system, and then add it to NetBeans.

Time for action – installing XDebug on Windows

The XDebug extension comes with the XAMPP bundle, by default. You just have to enable it from the loaded .ini file. Note that there could be multiple php.ini files present, and the file location can be different between different operating systems. So, let's try it...

1. Locate the loaded php.ini file from your phpinfo(), by pointing your browser to http://localhost/xampp/phpinfo.php.

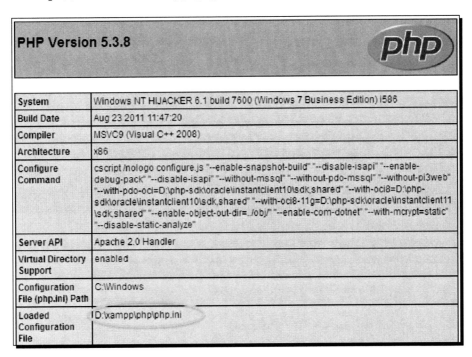

System	Windows NT HIJACKER 6.1 build 7600 (Windows 7 Business Edition) i586
Build Date	Aug 23 2011 11:47:20
Compiler	MSVC9 (Visual C++ 2008)
Architecture	x86
Configure Command	cscript /nologo configure.js "--enable-snapshot-build" "--disable-isapi" "--enable-debug-pack" "--disable-isapi" "--without-mssql" "--without-pdo-mssql" "--without-pi3web" "--with-pdo-oci=D:\php-sdk\oracle\instantclient10\sdk,shared" "--with-oci8=D:\php-sdk\oracle\instantclient10\sdk,shared" "--with-oci8-11g=D:\php-sdk\oracle\instantclient11\sdk,shared" "--enable-object-out-dir=../obj/" "--enable-com-dotnet" "--with-mcrypt=static" "--disable-static-analyze"
Server API	Apache 2.0 Handler
Virtual Directory Support	enabled
Configuration File (php.ini) Path	C:\Windows
Loaded Configuration File	D:\xampp\php\php.ini

You can see the loaded php.ini file located at D:\xampp\php\php.ini.

2. Open the php.ini file located at D:\xampp\php\php.ini, and find the following line:

```
[XDebug]
;zend_extension = "D:\xampp\php\ext\php_xdebug.dll"
```

3. Find and uncomment the following lines by removing the leading semicolon:

```
zend_extension = "D:\xampp\php\ext\php_xdebug.dll"
xdebug.remote_enable = 1
xdebug.remote_handler = "dbgp"
xdebug.remote_host = "localhost"
xdebug.remote_port = 9000
```

4. Save the `php.ini` file and restart your Apache web server from the XAMPP control panel, to enable the XDebug extension.

5. To verify whether the XDebug object is enabled or not, refresh your `phpinfo()` page and find XDebug enabled, as shown in the following screenshot:

xdebug

xdebug support		enabled	
Version		2.1.0rc1	

Supported protocols		Revision	
DBGp - Common DeBuGger Protocol		$Revision. 1.145 $	

Directive	Local Value	Master Value
xdebug.auto_trace	Off	Off
xdebug.collect_assignments	Off	Off
xdebug.collect_includes	On	On
xdebug.collect_params	0	0
xdebug.collect_return	Off	Off
xdebug.collect_vars	Off	Off

6. If you have XDebug enabled, it will override `var_dump()` in PHP. You may dump a variable like `var_dump($var)` inside your code, and the browser will display the enhanced `var_dump` as follows (strings are printed in red):

```
array
  0 => string '5' (length=1)
  'id' => string '5' (length=1)
  1 => string 'M A Hossain Tonu' (length=16)
  'name' => string 'M A Hossain Tonu' (length=16)
  2 => string 'tonu.jpg' (length=8)
  'image' => string 'tonu.jpg' (length=8)
  3 => string 'hello world' (length=11)
  'status' => string 'hello world' (length=11)
  4 => string '1319128088' (length=10)
  'timestamp' => string '1319128088' (length=10)
```

Bingo! You just loaded with XDebug in your development environment.

What just happened?

We have just enabled XDebug for our XAMPP bundle in Windows, and also verified the extension loaded with configurations. Note that such general steps to enable XDebug can be followed to enable other built-in extensions from php.ini. You just need to uncomment the extension at php.ini and restart your web server to make the change effective. Also, enabling XDebug in the LAMP or MAMP stack is pretty much similar.

 Always check the phpinfo() page for the loaded path of php.ini.

Enabling XDebug on Ubuntu

Enabling XDebug is quite easy in Ubuntu. We can install it via the **apt-get** package installer and update xdebug.ini for loaded configurations.

Time for action – installing XDebug on Ubuntu

From the console, run the following commands:

1. Install XDebug using the following command:

```
sudo apt-get install php5-xdebug
```

2. Update xdebug.ini using the gedit (in-built) editor.

```
sudo gedit /etc/php5/apache2/conf.d/xdebug.ini
```

3. Change xdebug.ini so that it looks as follows:

```
zend_extension=/usr/lib/php5/20090626+lfs/xdebug.so
xdebug.remote_enable=1
xdebug.remote_handler=dbgp
xdebug.remote_mode=req
xdebug.remote_host=127.0.0.1
xdebug.remote_port=9000
```

Note that the first line of these configurations may be available inside xdebug.ini, and you may have to add the remaining lines.

4. Restart Apache.

```
sudo service apache2 restart
```

5. Refresh the `phpinfo()` page, and find the latest XDebug installed with the version number.

What just happened?

We just enabled XDebug for our LAMP in Ubuntu and also verified the extension loaded with configurations. Note that such general steps to enable XDebug can be followed to enable other built-in extensions from `php.ini`. You just need to uncomment the extension at `php.ini` and restart your web server to make the change effective.

Enabling XDebug on Mac OS X

Modify the appropriate version of the loaded `php.ini` file to enable XDebug in Mac, uncomment the following lines, and restart the Apache server from the MAMP control panel.

```
[xdebug]
zend_extension="/Applications/MAMP/bin/php5.3/lib/php/extensions/no-
debug-non-zts-20090626/xdebug.so"
xdebug.remote_enable=on
xdebug.remote_handler=dbgp
xdebug.remote_host=localhost
xdebug.remote_port=9000
```

XDebug is now running on your Mac OSX. MAMP Pro users can easily edit `php.ini` from the MAMP Pro control panel, by selecting **File | Edit template | PHP 5.3.2 php.ini** from the menu.

Finally, we have XDebug enabled in our local development environment.

Debugging the PHP source with NetBeans

To proceed, we would like to check the required debugging settings for NetBeans. Select the **Tools | Options | PHP | Debugging** tab:

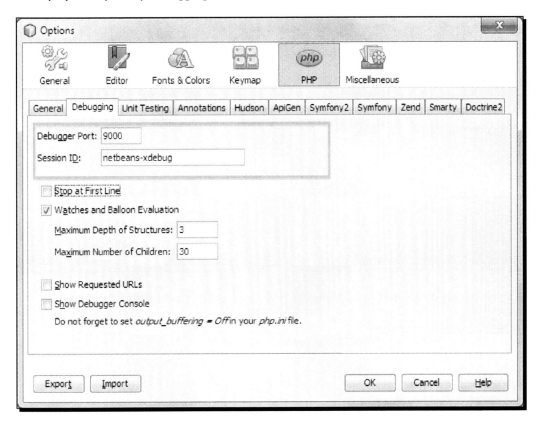

In this window, uncheck the **Stop at First Line** checkbox, because we want to stop at our desired line and check the **Watches and Balloon Evaluation** checkbox. This option enables you to watch custom expressions or variables while debugging.

Now, let's have a look into a debugging session running in the NetBeans window:

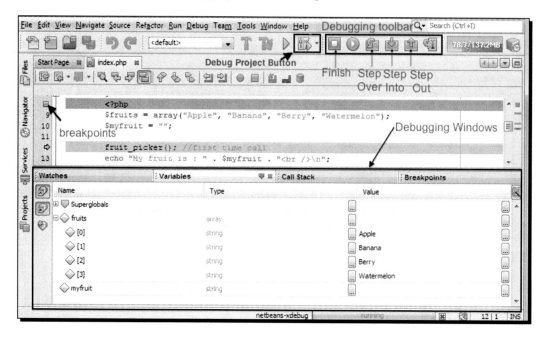

In this screenshot, the debug toolbar and button are indicated by functional names.

 Learn more about the debugging toolbar from
http://netbeans.org/kb/docs/php/debugging.html#work.

The debugger windows

When you start a debugging session, a set of debugger windows open below the main editor window. To add a new window, select **Window | Debugging**. The following windows are available:

◆ **Local Variables** shows a list of initialized variables, their types, and values

◆ **Watches** shows a list of user-defined expressions with their values

◆ **Calls Stack** shows a list of called functions in reverse order; the function called last is at the top of the list

◆ **Breakpoints** shows a list of files and numbers of the lines where breakpoints are set

◆ **Sessions** shows a list of currently active debugging sessions

◆ The **Threads** window indicates which PHP script is currently active and whether it is suspended at a breakpoint or running. If the script is running, you need to go to the browser window and interact with the script.

◆ The **Sources** window displays all the files and scripts loaded for the debugging session. The Sources window does not currently function for PHP projects.

Basic debugging workflow

Here are the basic debugging workflows:

1. The user sets a breakpoint at the line where the PHP source code execution should be paused.

2. When that line is reached, the user executes the script one line after another, by pressing the *F7* and *F8* buttons, and checks the values of the variables.

 See *Appendix* for NetBeans IDE keyboard shortcuts for debugging and testing.

Time for action – running a debugging session

This section illustrates standard debugging sessions, and we will create a sample project to practice debugging on it:

1. Create a NetBeans PHP project. For our example, we name it `chapter4`.

2. Type the following code in the `index.php` file:

```php
<?php

$fruits = array("Apple", "Banana", "Berry", "Watermelon");
$myfruit = "";

fruit_picker(); //first time call
echo "My fruit is : " . $myfruit . "<br />\n";
fruit_picker(); //second time call
echo "My fruit is now: " . $myfruit . "<br />\n";
fruit_picker(); //third time call
echo "My fruit is finally: " . $myfruit . "<br />\n";

function fruit_picker () {
    Global $myfruit, $fruits;
    $myfruit = $fruits[rand(0, 3)];
}
?>
```

The previous code contains:

- A `$fruits` array containing fruit names.
- A variable `$myfruit`, which contains a single fruit name as a string, initially with an empty string.
- A method `fruit_picker()`, which picks a fruit name from the `$fruits` array on a random basis and changes the value of `$myfruit`. Also, `$fruits` and `$myfruit` are defined as `Global` inside the function, so that the function can use and modify them within their global scope.

3. To test the debugging steps, we can set a breakpoint by pressing *Ctrl+F8* at the beginning of the PHP block, as shown in the following screenshot, or simply click on the line number of that line, to add the breakpoint:

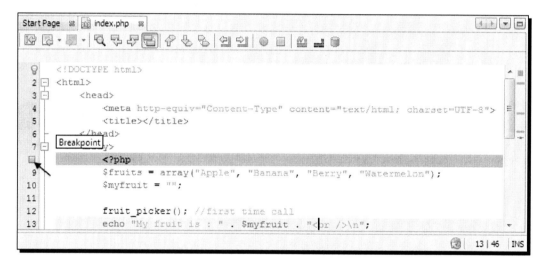

4. To start the debugging session, press *Ctrl+F5*, or click on the **Debug Project (chapter4)** button from the **Debug** toolbar, or right-click on the project name and choose **Debug** in the projects window. The debugger will stop at the breakpoint. The browser opens in a page-loading mode with the project debug URL, which is `http://localhost/chapter4/index.php?XDEBUG_SESSION_START=netbeans-xdebug`.

5. Press *F7* three times to step into the third execution point from the breakpoint. The debugger stops at the line where the function `fruit_picker()` is called for the first time. The **Variables** window shows the variables `$fruits` and `$myfruit` with their values similar to the following screenshot:

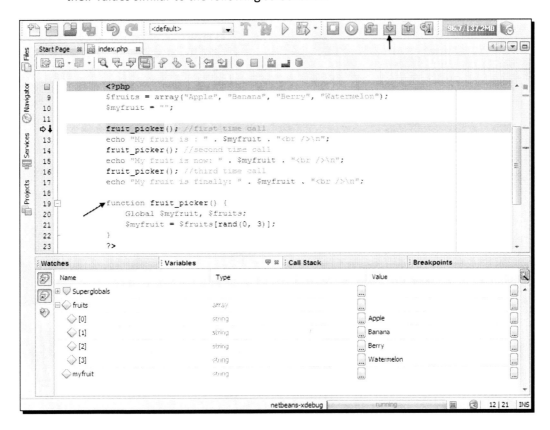

At our code, you can see that the `fruit_picker()` function is going to be called three times consecutively.

6. To step into the `fruit_picker()` function, press *F7*, and the debugger will start to execute the code inside `fruit_picker()`, as shown in the following screenshot:

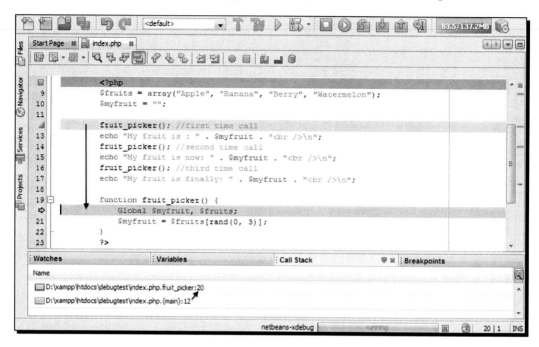

7. Press *F7* two times, and the `fruit_picker()` execution will end. Now, check the new value of `$myfruit` at the **Variables** window:

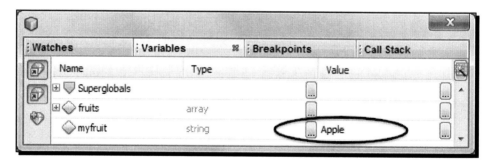

8. Again, press *F7* three times to step into the `fruit_picker()` function from the line where it has been called for the second time. As you have already verified that the function is working perfectly, you may want to cancel the function execution. To **Step Out** and return to the next line, press *Ctrl+F7*.

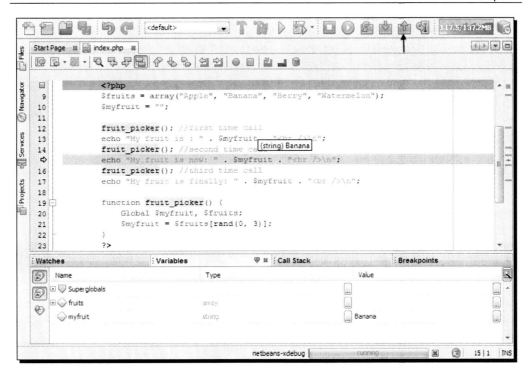

Note that the value of `$myfruit` keeps changing, and you can hover on that variable to view it.

9. As you just checked and found that your code is working correctly, you can step over the current line by pressing *F8*.

10. Finally, you can go through the next lines by pressing *F7*, or step over by pressing *F8* and reach to the end. Again, press *Shift+F5* or click on the **Finish Debugger Session** button, if you wish to finish the session. At the end of the session, the browser displays the result (code output) of the session.

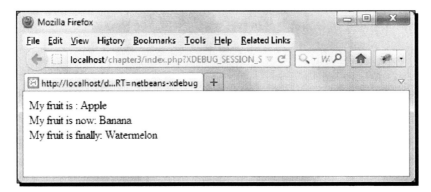

What just happened?

Practicing for the debugging session has been done, and hopefully we got a grip on debugging, using NetBeans. You can also add multiple breakpoints to follow up your program execution. So in this way, you can track all the variables, expressions, method calling sequences, program control jumping, and so on in your program. This is the process of finding what is going wrong inside the code. Mainly, you are now prepared to conquer some unwanted situations or bugs, while coding.

Adding Watches

To observe an expression in your code execution, adding the watch expression can help you catch an error. Now, let's have some fun...

Time for action – adding the expression to watch

As an example, we want to test whether the same fruit name was picked again or not, by the `fruit_picker()` function. We may save the `$myfruit` value each time before a new random fruit name pick, and compare these two fruit names using an expression. So, let's add the expression watcher by using the following steps:

1. Modify the `fruit_picker()` function as follows:

```
function fruit_picker() {
    Global $myfruit, $fruits;
    $old_fruit = $myfruit;
    $myfruit = $fruits[rand(0, 3)];
}
```

   We just added the line `$old_fruit = $myfruit;` to preserve the previous value of `$myfruit`, so that we can compare the previous pick in `$old_fruit` and the new pick in `$myfruit` at end of the function. We actually want to check if the same fruit was picked.

2. Select **Debug | New Watch** or press *Ctrl+Shift+F7*. The **New Watch** window is opened.

3. Enter the following expression and click on **OK**.

```
($old_fruit == $myfruit)
```

We will observe this expression outcome at the closing brace (}) of the `fruit_picker()` function. If the expression yields (bool) 1 at the function closing brace, then we will know if the new picked fruit is the same as the old one, or the same fruit was picked again. The added watch expression can be found listed in both the **Watches** and **Variables** window.

4. Run the debugging session, as shown in the previous section. When the debugger stops at the closing brace of the `fruit_picker()` function, check that the expression value is (bool) 0 if the new pick is different from the old one, and the value is (bool) 1 if it's the same consecutive pick again.

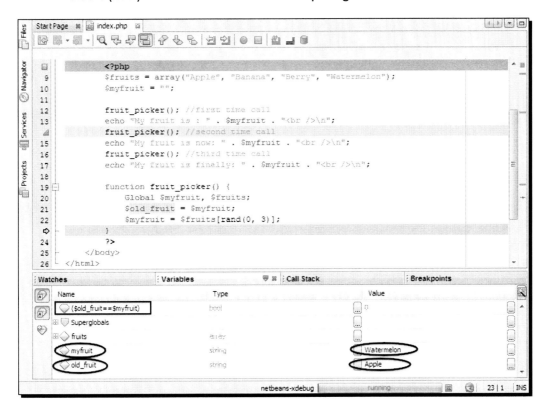

In this way, you can keep watching an expression to hunt for a bug.

What just happened?

Adding the watch expression to the debugging session was fun. You can add multiple watches to analyze some programming flaws. Simply, debugging enables you to look inside variables, functions, expressions, execution flows, and so on, so one can easily spot the bug and clean it.

 See *Appendix* for NetBeans IDE keyboard shortcuts for debugging and testing.

Pop quiz – debugging with XDebug

1. Which of the following are XDebug features?
   a. Automatic stack trace upon error
   b. Automatic bug fixing
   c. Function call logging
   d. Enhanced `var_dump()`

2. What will happen when a breakpoint occurs in NetBeans?
   a. The IDE will jump over the breakpoint and display the result
   b. The IDE will stop code execution at that point, allowing you to see what is going on in the windows debugging
   c. The IDE will terminate the debugging session and reset the results of the windows being debugged
   d. None of the above

3. What is the purpose of Watches?
   a. Displaying the time in NetBeans
   b. Observing expressions in your code execution
   c. Observing expression timings
   d. Inspecting a debugging session

Have a go hero – exploring NetBeans debugging feature

In the **Debugging** window, enable the feature called **Show Requested URLs**. When it has been enabled, a new **Output** window will occur during debugging, and the currently processed URLs will be shown there. Also, enable another **Output** window called **PHP Debugger Console** to see the output for your debugged scripts in it. Remember to set `output_buffering = Off` in your `php.ini` file, to see it immediately.

Testing with PHPUnit

Source code testing is essential in the test-driven development approach. Testing depicts the way to check whether the code behaves as expected or not, with a set of runnable code fragments. Unit testing tests the correctness of parts (units) of the software, whose runnable code-fragments are called **Unit Tests**. NetBeans IDE supports automated unit tests using **PHPUnit** and the **Selenium** test framework.

Configuring PHPUnit

As we run XAMPP in the Windows box, it provides a built-in PHPUnit package. Note that if your project is running in PHP 5.3, then you should use PHPUnit 3.4.0 or newer. In our case, the latest XAMPP 1.7.7 (with PHP 5.3.8) stack has PHPUnit 2.3.6 installed inside it, which is not compatible with PHP 5.3. You also need to upgrade the existing **PHP Extension and Application Repository** (**PEAR**) installation to install the latest PHPUnit and required PEAR packages as well.

To check the version of the installed PEAR, PHP, and Zend engine, browse to the PHP installation directory D:\xampp\php from the command prompt or Terminal, and enter the pear version command, which will give you the following output:

```
PEAR Version: 1.7.2
PHP Version: 5.3.8
Zend Engine Version: 2.3.0
Running on: Windows NT….
```

So it's time to install the latest PHPUnit. In order to do that, PEAR should be upgraded first.

Time for action – installing PHPUnit via PEAR

In the following steps, we will upgrade PEAR and install PHPUnit via PEAR, for the corresponding environments:

1. Run the command prompt as an administrator, go to the PHP installation directory where the pear.bat file belongs (D:\xampp\php), and execute the following command:

   ```
   pear upgrade pear
   ```

   This upgrades the existing PEAR installation. In Ubuntu or Mac OS X system, run the following command:

   ```
   sudo pear upgrade pear
   ```

In the case of MAMP, if you encounter the error `sudo: pear: command not found`, then refer to the section *Configuring MAMP issues*.

2. To install the latest PHPUnit, type the following two commands:

```
pear config-set auto_discover 1
pear install pear.phpunit.de/PHPUnit
```

It discovers the download channels automatically and installs the latest PHPUnit along with the available packages.

3. To check the PHPUnit installation, run the following command:

```
phpunit -version
```

You will see a command similar to the following:

```
PHPUnit 3.6.10 by Sebastian Bergmann.
```

4. To list the remote packages for PHPUnit, run the following command:

```
pear remote-list -c phpunit
```

What just happened?

We have upgraded the PEAR installation using the `pear upgrade pear` command. We enabled the PEAR channel, auto discover configuration, and the latest PHPUnit has been installed using these automatic installation channels. Other PHP extensions can be installed easily from the extension repository in this way.

Again, if you have upgraded your PEAR installation and had enabled the auto discover feature earlier, then only the command `pear install pear.phpunit.de/PHPUnit` would have accomplished the PHPUnit installation.

Run the command prompt as an administrator in Windows, to ease directory permissions. You may right-click on the program and select **Run as Administrator**.

Configuring MAMP issues

In the case of MAMP, while using PEAR commands from Terminal, if you encounter the error `pear: command not found`, then running `which php` will point us to the OS X's default version.

```
$ pear
-bash: pear: command not found

$ which php
/usr/bin/php
```

You may then need to fix it. To rectify this, we need to add PHP's bin directory to our path. PATH is an environment variable that denotes which directories to look in for the commands. PATH can be modified by editing the .profile file under your home directory. We've used the PHP5.3 bin version path for this tutorial, but you can choose from whatever versions are available to you.

From Terminal, run the following command to add the desired PHP's bin directory, to use php, pear, and other relevant executable files from that directory:

```
$ echo "export PATH=/Applications/MAMP/bin/php/php5.3/bin:$PATH" >>
~/.profile
```

As you can see, a line is added to the .profile file inside the user's home directory, which includes the php5.3 bin directory path to the environment variable PATH.

Now, stop MAMP and change the files' permissions with the following commands, to make those files executable:

```
chmod 774 /Applications/MAMP/bin/php5.3/bin/pear
chmod 774 /Applications/MAMP/bin/php5.3/bin/php
```

The chmod command changes the file mode or access control list. 774 means the file "owner" and "group" of the file users will be permitted to read, write, and execute the file. Everyone else will only be able to read it, but not write or execute the file.

While writing, the latest MAMP 1.9 version comes with a corrupt pear.conf file for PHP versions. So, rename that file to prevent it from loading to the system, using the following command:

```
mv /Applications/MAMP/conf/php5.3/pear.conf /Applications/MAMP/conf/
php5.3/backup_pear.conf
```

Actually, inside the given pear.conf file, the PHP path strings contain php5 instead of php5.3 or php5.2.

Now, start MAMP again and restart your Terminal session. Hence, MAMP issues are fixed, and you can test it by running which php or which pear commands from Terminal. In order to install PHPUnit using MAMP, you can now proceed with *step 1* of the *Time for action – Installing PHPUnit via PEAR* section of this chapter.

Adding PHPUnit to NetBeans

To make PHPUnit the default unit tester with NetBeans IDE, select the **Tools | Options | PHP Tab | Unit Testing** tab, use **Search** to enter the PHPUnit `.bat` script path automatically in the **PHPUnit script** field, and click on **OK**.

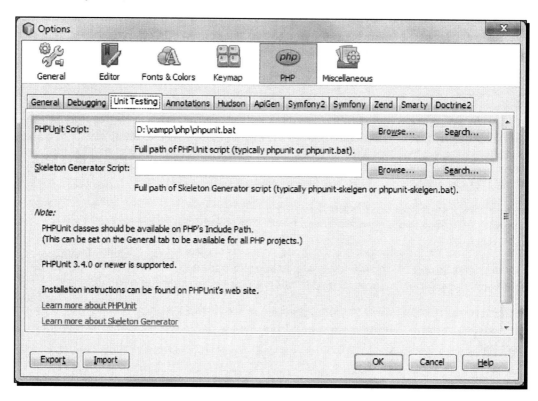

Again, for Mac OS X, the PHPUnit path will be similar to `/Applications/MAMP/bin/php5.3/bin/phpunit`.

Pop quiz – PEAR

1. What does PEAR stand for?

    a. PHP Extended Application Repository

    b. PHP Extension and Application Repository

    c. PHP Extension Community Library

    d. PHP Extra Applicable Repository

Creating and running PHPUnit tests

In this section, we will learn to create and run PHPUnit tests. NetBeans IDE can create test scripts and run PHPUnit tests on all PHP classes in a file. The IDE automates test script generation and the entire test process. To be sure that the test script generator will work, name the PHP file the same as the first class in the file.

Time for action – testing with PHPUnit

In this tutorial, we will create a new NetBeans project to test our PHP classes from the IDE using PHPUnit. In order to do this, follow the steps below:

1. Create a new project named `Calculator`, add a PHP class named `Calculator` in the project (right-click on project node and select **New | PHP Class**, then insert the class name), and type the following code for the `Calculator` class:

```php
<?php
class Calculator {

  public function add($a, $b) {
    return $a + $b;
  }
}
?>
```

You can see that the `add()` method simply performs the addition of two numbers and returns the sum. We will test this method unit, to see whether it is returning the correct sum or not.

2. Add a comment block with the `@assert` annotations and some sample input and output as shown in the following code. Note that one incorrect assertion is included in the following example:

```php
<?php
class Calculator {
    /**
     * @assert  (0, 0)  == 0
     * @assert  (0, 1)  == 1
     * @assert  (1, 0)  == 1
     * @assert  (1, 1)  == 2
     * @assert  (1, 2)  == 4
     */
public function add($a, $b) {
    return $a + $b;
    }
}
?>
```

3. In the **Projects** window, right-click on the `Calculator.php` node and select **Tools | Create PHPUnit Tests**. Note that you can create tests for all the files in a project using the context menu in the **Source Files** node.

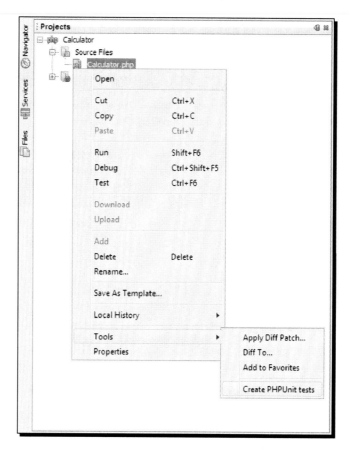

4. The first time you create tests, a dialog box opens asking you for the directory in which you want to store test scripts. In this example, the **Browse** function (button) may be used to create a `tests` directory.

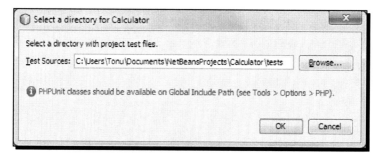

We may keep the test files separate from the source folder. Also, if you wish to exclude those test scripts from future-source versioning, you may keep them separate.

5. The IDE generates a test class in a file called `CalculatorTest.php`, which appears in your **Projects** window and opens in the editor.

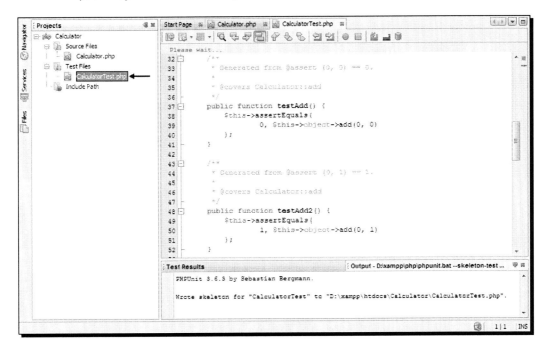

Note that test methods have been created for each `@assert` annotation inside the class.

6. To test the `Calculator.php` file, right-click on the file's node and select **Test**, or press *Ctrl+F6*. The IDE runs the tests and displays the results in the **Test Results** window.

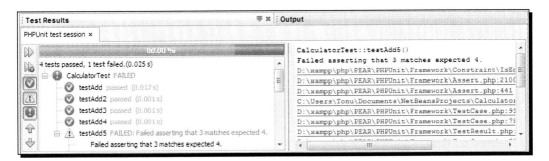

As you can see, because of an incorrect input, one of the tests has failed. This is marked with a yellow exclamation sign in the **Test Results** window. Also, you can see the number of passed and failed tests. So, the overall passed tests percentage (denoted with a green bar) can be obtained.

7. Note that you can run the test for the whole project also. Right-click on the project's node and select **Test**, or press *Alt+F6*. Consider checking the **Output** window as well, for more verbose textual output.

What just happened?

PHP classes or projects can be tested in parts, using PHPUnit. The best part here is that you don't need to bother about generating test scripts and showing the test results in a graphical way, as IDE takes care of it. You can learn more about PHPUnit tests at `http://www.phpunit.de/manual/current/en/`.

 Learn more examples of assertions at `http://www.phpunit.de/manual/current/en/writing-tests-for-phpunit.html#writing-tests-for-phpunit.assertions`.

Dealing with code coverage with PHPUnit

NetBeans IDE provides a code coverage feature with the help of PHPUnit. Code coverage checks whether all your methods have been covered by PHPUnit tests. In this section, we will see how code coverage works with our existing `Calculator` class.

Time for action – using code coverage

Follow the steps below to see how the code coverage feature works in NetBeans:

1. Open `Calculator.php`, add a duplicate `add` function, and name it `add2`. The `Calculator` class now looks similar to the following:

```php
<?php

class Calculator {

    /**
     * @assert (0, 0) == 0
     * @assert (0, 1) == 1
     * @assert (1, 0) == 1
     * @assert (1, 1) == 2
     * @assert (1, 2) == 4
```

```
    */
public function add($a, $b) {
    return $a + $b;
    }

public function add2($a, $b) {
    return $a + $b;
    }

}

?>
```

2. Right-click on the project node. From the **Context** menu, select **Code Coverage | Collect and Display Code Coverage**. By default, the **Show Editor Bar** is also selected.

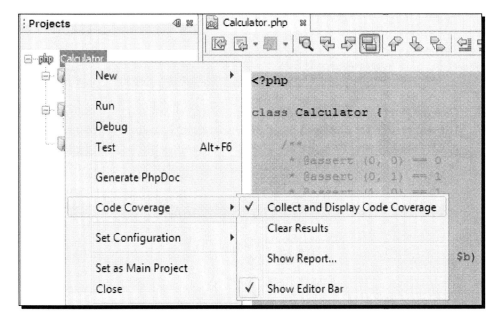

3. The editor now has a code coverage editor bar across the bottom. Since code coverage has not been tested, the editor bar reports 0.0% coverage (it also displays such a percentage after you click on **Clear** to clear the test results).

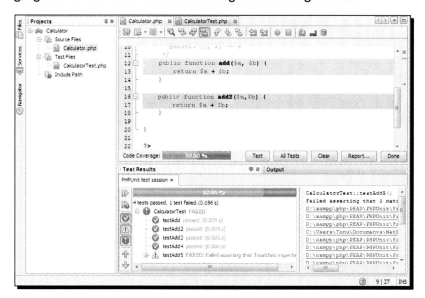

4. Click on **Test** to test the opened file or **All Tests** to run all the tests for the project. The test results are displayed. In addition, the **Code Coverage** bar tells you what percentages of your total methods have been covered by tests. In the editor window, the covered code is highlighted in green, and the uncovered code is highlighted in red. Check out the following code coverage session:

5. In the **Code Coverage** bar, click on **Report....** The **Code Coverage** report opens, showing the results of all the tests that were run on your project. Buttons in the bar let you clear the results, run all the tests again, and deactivate code coverage (click on **Done**).

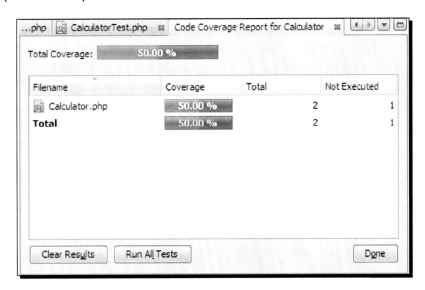

As you can see, the add2() method hasn't been covered with the unit tests, so the report shows 50% code coverage, otherwise it would have showed 100% coverage.

What just happened?

We have finished using the NetBeans code coverage feature with PHPUnit, so we can determine which units are not covered by PHPUnit tests. So, code coverage can be applied when you create PHPUnit tests for your code units and want to be assured that all units have been covered by tests. However, a maximum code coverage percentage is expected.

 Refactor test scripts when you refactor codes.

Testing using the Selenium framework

Selenium is a portable software-testing framework for web applications and automated browsers. Primarily, it is for automating web applications for testing purposes across many platforms. NetBeans IDE has a plugin that includes a Selenium server. With this plugin, you can run Selenium tests on PHP, web applications, or Maven projects. To run Selenium tests on PHP, you need to install the **Testing_Selenium** package to your PHP environment.

Installing Selenium

As we have upgraded PEAR and installed the latest PHPUnit, we should already have `Testing_Selenium-beta` installed along with them. To check the Selenium installation, run the following command from Terminal, and you will be able to view the installed version:

```
pear info Testing_Selenium-beta
```

Otherwise, run the following command to have Selenium installed:

```
pear install Testing_Selenium-0.4.4
```

Time for action – running tests with Selenium

Let's run tests with Selenium through the following steps:

1. To install the plugin, open **Tools | Plugins**, and install **Selenium Module** for PHP.

2. In the **Projects** window, right-click on the project node for your **Calculator** project. Select **New | Other**. The **New File** wizard is opened. Select **Selenium** and click on **Next**.

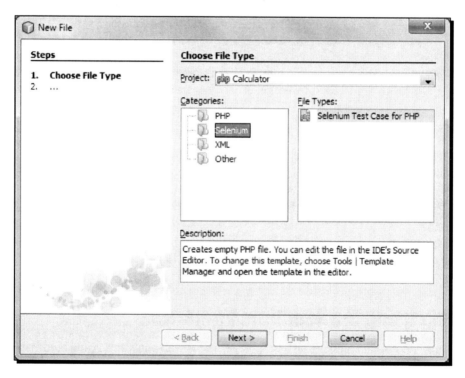

The first time you create a Selenium test, a dialog box opens, asking you to set a directory for the Selenium test files. This should be a separate directory from the PHPUnit test files; otherwise, the Selenium tests will run every time you run unit tests. Running functional tests, such as Selenium, usually takes more time than running unit tests. Therefore, you will probably not want to run these tests every time you run unit tests.

3. Accept the defaults in the **Name** and **Location** pages, and click on **Finish**. The new Selenium test file is opened in the editor and also appears in the **Projects** window.

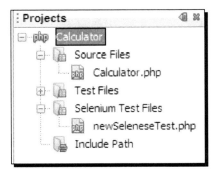

4. The **Run Selenium Tests** item is now added to the project's context menu. Click on this item, and the Selenium test results are displayed in the **Test Results** window, which is the same as the PHPUnit tests.

You can also modify the Selenium server's settings. The Selenium server is added as a new server in the **Services** tab.

What just happened?

We just traded the testing using the Selenium testing framework for PHP applications. It provides testing support for developers over multiple OSes, browsers, and programming languages, and allows in recording, editing, and debugging tests. Simply, this is a complete testing solution for testers. You can evolve your test with your evolving code structure using Selenium. The software is based on the PHPUnit framework and inherits much of its functionality.

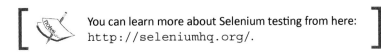

You can learn more about Selenium testing from here:
`http://seleniumhq.org/`.

Pop quiz – unit testing and code coverage

1. What is unit testing?

    a. Testing the smallest testable parts of the code

    b. Testing the individual methods of a class

    c. Testing, where you know the input, and what the output will be

    d. All of the above

2. Which assertion will fail the test of subtracting two numbers?

    a. `@assert (0, 0) == 0`

    b. `@assert (2, 3) == -1`

    c. `@assert (4, 2) == 3`

    d. `@assert (5, 1) == 4`

3. If six tests were passed and four tests were failed while testing units in a class consisting of a single method, then what will be the code coverage percentage?

    a. 60%

    b. 50%

    c. 100%

    d. 40%

4. Which is not a feature of test framework Selenium?

    a. Automating browsers

    b. Finding defects missed by manual testing

    c. Observing an expression

    d. Unlimited iterations of test case execution

Have a go hero – learning test dependencies

One unit test usually covers one function or method and can be dependent on other unit tests as well. Now, use the `@depends` annotation to express unit test dependencies and practice with the help of `http://www.phpunit.de/manual/current/en/writing-tests-for-phpunit.html#writing-tests-for-phpunit.test-dependencies`.

 See *Appendix* for NetBeans IDE keyboard shortcuts for debugging and testing.

Summary

In this chapter, we have learned to debug and test PHP applications using NetBeans. The IDE has been integrated in an effective way with those debugging and testing tools. Also, for automated tests, the generated scripts made the process hassle free and easy.

Specifically, we have focused on:

- XDebug configuration on various OSes
- Running the debugging session with NetBeans and XDebug
- Installing PHPUnit
- Unit testing using PHPUnit
- Code coverage using PHPUnit and NetBeans
- Introducing the Selenium test framework using NetBeans

Life is now easier with debugging and testing tools. In the next chapter, we will emphasize source and API documentation to make our source code more understandable.

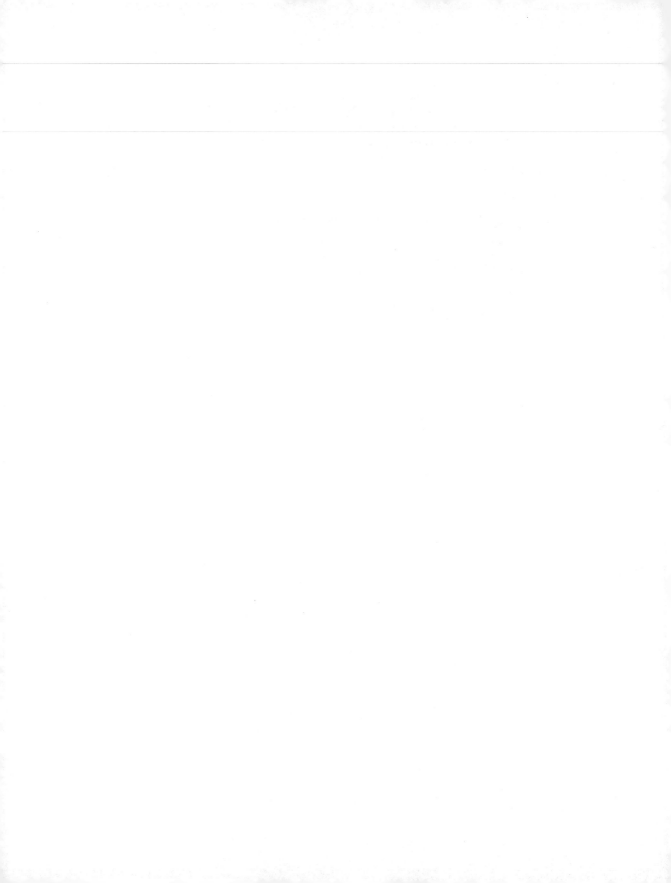

5
Using Code Documentation

Code tells you how, comments tell you why - Jeff Atwood

In this chapter, we are going to document our PHP source code using the NetBeans IDE. We will learn how to quickly document variables, methods, classes, or the entire project, and discuss the following issues:

- ◆ Convention for source documentation
- ◆ How to document the source code
- ◆ PHP project API documentation

Writing great documentation

Coding is the art of instructing machines, and when it comes to human readability, code should be expressive, self-explanatory, and beautiful. The code should be reusable and understandable, so that you can use it again a couple of months from now. A good practitioner makes the code as simple as possible to understand, and keeps the code documentation where it is really required.

Code documentation is the motivating part of coding, particularly when you are working in a collaborative team environment; documentation should be done in a sensible way, so that learning the intent of the code can be faster among collaborators.

A regular practice to document the source code is putting comments in your code specified by the **PHPDoc** format, so that your code becomes more meaningful and the external documentation generator can parse such comments.

PHPDoc – commenting standard for PHP

PHPDoc is an adaptation of Javadoc for the PHP programming language. Since it is the standard for commenting the PHP code, it allows external document generators, such as phpDocumentor and ApiGen to generate HTML documentation for APIs. It helps a variety of IDEs, such as NetBeans, PhpStorm, Zend Studio, and Aptana Studio, to interpret variable types and provide improved code completion, type hinting, and debugging. According to PHPDoc, documentation is written using text blocks named **DocBlock**, which precede the element to be documented. As a way of describing programming constructs such as class, interface, functions, methods, and so on, tag annotations are used inside the DocBlock.

Example of a DocBlock

A DocBlock is an extended C++ style PHP comment that begins with "/**" and has "*" at the beginning of every line.

```
/**
 * This is a DocBlock comment
 */
```

A DocBlock contains three basic segments, in this order:

- Short description
- Long description
- Tags

Example:

```
/**
 * Short description
 *
 * Long description first sentence starts here
 * and continues on this line for a while
 * finally concluding here at the end of
 * this paragraph
 *
 * The blank line above denotes a paragraph break
 */
```

The short description starts on the first line, and can be terminated with a blank line or a period. A period inside a word (for example `example.com` or `0.1 %`) is ignored. If the short description becomes more than three lines long, then only the first line is taken. The long description continues for as many lines as required, and may contain the HTML markup for display formatting. The external document parser will convert all the whitespaces into a single space in the long description, and may use paragraph breaks to define newlines, or `<pre>`, as discussed in the following section.

The long and short description of a DocBlock is parsed for a few selected HTML tags, which determine additional formatting using the followings tags:

- `<b>`: This tag is used to emphasize/bold the text
- `<code>`: This tag is used to surround the PHP code; some converters will highlight it
- `<br>`: This tag is used to provide a hard-line break, and may be ignored by some converters
- `<i>`: This tag is used to italicize/mark the text as important
- `<kbd>`: This tag is used to denote the keyboard input/screen display
- `<li>`: This tag is used to list items
- `<ol>`: This tag is used to create an ordered list
- `<ul>`: This tag is used to create an unordered list
- `<p>`: This tag is used to enclose all the paragraphs; otherwise, content will be considered text
- `<pre>`: This tag is used to preserve line breaks and spacing, and assumes all tags are text (like XML's CDATA)
- `<samp>`: This tag is used to denote samples or examples (non-PHP)
- `<var>`: This tag is used to denote a variable name

In rare cases when the text "`<b>`" is needed in a DocBlock, use a double delimiter, as in `<<b>>`. The external document generator will automatically translate that to the physical text "`<b>`".

Acquainting with PHPDoc tags

PHPDoc tags are single words prefixed by an @ symbol, and are only parsed if they are the first thing on the new line of a DocBlock. A DocBlock precedes before structural elements, and such elements can be programming constructs, such as namespaces, classes, interfaces, traits, functions, methods, properties, constants, and variables.

Some common lists of tags with details have been divided into groups for better understanding, as follows:

Data type tags

Tag	Usage	Description
@param	Type [$varname] description	Documents a function or method parameter.
@return	Type description	Documents the return type of a function or method. This tag should not be used for constructors or methods defined with a void return type.
@var	Type	Documents the data type for a class variable or constant.

Legal tags

Tag	Usage	Description
@author	Author name <author@email>	Documents the author of the current element
@copyright	Name date	Documents copyright information
@license	URL name	Is used to indicate which license is applicable for the associated structural elements

Versioning tags

Tag	Usage	Description
@version	Version string	Provides the version number of a class or method
@since	Version string	Documents the release version
@deprecated	Version description	Is used to indicate which elements are deprecated and are to be removed in a future version
@todo	Information string	Documents things that need to be done to the code at a later date

Other tags

Tag	Usage	Description
@example	/path/to/example	Documents the location of an external saved example file
@link	URL link text	Documents the URL reference
@see	Element name(s) separated by comma	Documents any element
@uses	Name of element	Documents how the element is used
@package	Name of a package	Documents a group of related classes and functions
@subpackage	Name of sub package	Documents a group of related classes and functions

Among the most used tags, @param and @return can be used only for functions and methods, @var for properties and constants, @package and @subpackage for procedural pages or classes, while other tags, such as @author, @version, and so on, can be used for any element. Besides these tags, @example and @link can be used as inline tags.

You can find the list of tags at http://www.phpdoc.org/docs/latest/for-users/list-of-tags.html.

Now, we will dive into documenting our PHP source code using NetBeans.

Documenting the source code

In this section, we will learn to document functions, methods, classes, interfaces, global variables, constants, and so on, and discuss the benefits of using such a code documentation. As discussed earlier, in the collaborative development environment, the description of methods, classes, and so on, are very important to learn the intent of the code, and we will see that implemented practically in this section.

Now, create a new PHP project named Chapter5 in NetBeans, and use it for all the following tutorials.

Documenting the functions and methods

In this section, we will learn to use the NetBeans auto documentation feature at the beginning of a PHP function or method.

Time for action – documenting a PHP function or method

In this tutorial, let's create a simple PHP function or method with some parameters passed into it and different types of variables declared inside it. We are just practicing to see how the NetBeans auto documentation generator works on such commonly used structural elements. Let's go through the following steps:

1. Add a PHP file named `sample1.php` into the project, and type a PHP function as follows:

    ```php
    function testFunc(DateTime $param1, $param2, string $param3 =
    NULL)
    {
        $number = 7;

        return $number;
    }
    ```

    In this function we can see that there are three parameters passed into the `testFunc` method—`$param1` as `DateTime`, `$param2` without type-hinting as it may have a mixed type of value, and `$param3` is optional with a default `NULL` value. Also, inside the body, the function contains one integer type variable and returns that integer type as well.

2. Type `/**` in the line before the `testFunc` function, and press *Enter*. You can see that NetBeans parses the function and generates the documentation before the function according to the PHPDoc standard, which looks similar to the following:

    ```php
    /**
     *
     * @param DateTime $param1
     * @param type $param2
     * @param string $param3
     * @return int
     */
    function testFunc(DateTime $param1, $param2, string $param3 =
    NULL)
    {
        $number = 7;

        return $number;
    }
    ```

In the previous code snippet, we can see that NetBeans generated the documentation mentioning the parameters and return type, which are listed as follows:

- Parameters are annotated with the @param tag and parameter type from the given type hinting
- The return type is annotated with @return

You can see that the type and name beside each tag are separated with a whitespace. In case the type hint is unavailable, then NetBeans leaves it as a simple type, such as $param2. The word that is usually used in documentation is "mixed" when the real data type is unknown and you can edit that "type" as well.

3. You can add a description of each variable in the documentation; beside the variable name, just put the description with a leading whitespace as follows:

```
/**
 *
 * @param DateTime $param1 this is parameter1
 * @param array $param2 this is parameter2
 * @param string $param3 this is parameter3 which is optional
 * @return int what is returned, goes here
 */
```

4. Also, you may want to add a short description for the documentation, which looks similar to the following:

```
/**
 * a short description goes here
 *
 * @param DateTime $param1 this is parameter1
 * @param array $param2 this is parameter2
 * @param string $param3 this is parameter3 which is optional
 * @return int what is returned, goes here
 */
```

5. Now, let's see how this NetBeans-generated documentation looks, while someone tries to call this `testFunc` from anywhere within the project. Try to type the function name anywhere. Say, let's start typing the function name in the `index.php` file inside the project, and you will see the NetBeans auto-suggestion of that function name with parameter hints and the documentation, as follows:

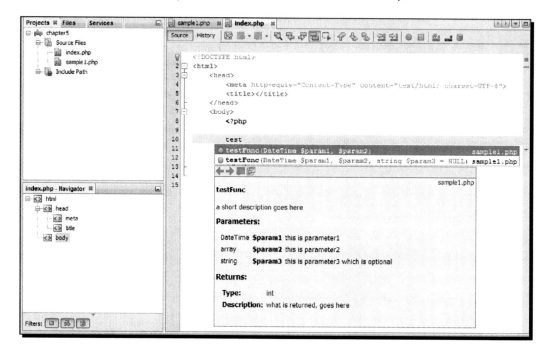

If documentation is available for a function or any element, then NetBeans shows the documentation while auto-suggestion is in process, as shown in the previous screenshot.

What just happened?

We just learned how to use the NetBeans auto documentation generator. By typing /** and pressing *Enter* before the functions, we can parse the metadata and generate the documentation. We can update the documentation as well. Again, the external document generator can extract such DocBlocks to create the project API documentation. Now, we will add a documentation before a PHP class in the next section.

Documenting classes

A document before a class is very important to learn about the class and its usage. A best practice is to decorate the preceding documentation with proper annotations, such as @ package, @author, @copyright, @license, @link, and @version, and with a proper description of the class.

Time for action – documenting the PHP class and class variables

In this section, we will add a PHP class using NetBeans and update the preceding DocBlock with class documentation tags. So let's go for it...

1. Right-click on the Chapter5 project to choose **New | PHP Class...**, insert the class name as Test into the **File Name** box, and click on **Finish**, as follows:

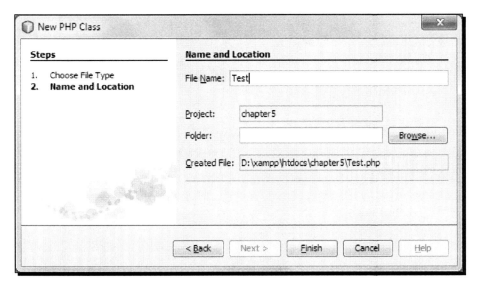

2. The `Test` class should look similar to the following:

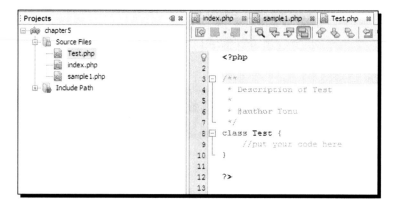

In the previous screenshot, you can see that the opened `Test` class has an added DocBlock at the top with a sample class description along with the `@author` tag.

3. You may want to add PHPDoc tags before the line containing the `@author` tag; say you want to add the `@package` tag as soon as you type `@p`. The NetBeans code auto completion feature shows tags starting with `@p` to have a description that looks similar to the following screenshot:

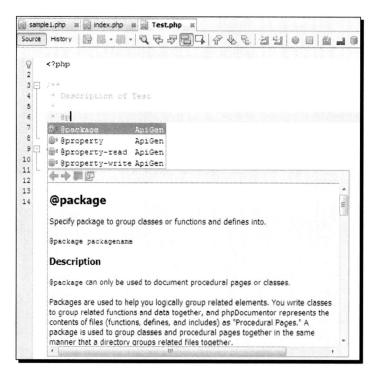

4. Update the DocBlock with your own, so it looks similar to the following:

```
/**
 * Short description of the Test Class
 *
 * Long multiline description of the Test Class goes here
 *
 * Note: any notes required
 * @package Chapter5
 * @author M A Hossain Tonu
 * @version 1.0
 * @copyright never
 * @link http://mahtonu.wordpress.com
 */
```

5. In the above documentation, you can see that corresponding tags have been added for the class, so that the class information is available while you try to instantiate the class object with code completion, as follows:

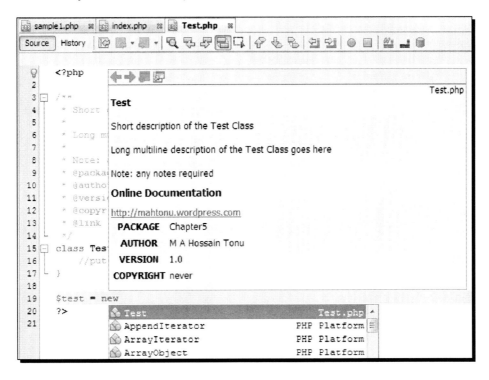

Also, such a class DocBlock can be extracted using the external API documentation generator.

6. Now, type a class variable named `$variable` into the `Test` class as follows:

```
public $variable;
```

7. To add the class variable documentation, type `/**`, and hit *Enter* before the line in which it is declared, so that the documentation looks similar to the following:

```
/**
 *
 * @var type
 */
```

8. Here, you may update the block as follows:

```
/**
 * example of documenting a variable's type
 * @var string
 */
```

9. In order to view the class hierarchy tree, at a later section, you may add a child class in our project named `TestChild` extending the `Test` class, which looks similar to the following:

```
/**
 * Short description of the TestChild Class
 *
 * Long multiline description of the TestChild Class goes here
 *
 * Note: any notes required
 * @package Chapter5
 * @author M A Hossain Tonu
 * @version 1.0
 * @copyright never
 * @link http://mahtonu.wordpress.com
 */
class TestChild extends Test {

}
```

What just happened?

We have practiced how to add documentation before PHP functions, classes, and its attributes using the PHPDoc format, and tested how this documented information becomes available throughout the project. The same style of DocBlock or appropriate tags can be applicable to document the PHP interfaces as well.

Documenting TODO tasks

You can use the `@todo` tag for an element, to document planned changes, which have not been implemented yet, and the tag may be used for almost any element that can be documented (global variable, constant, function, method, define, class, and variable).

Time for action – using @todo tags

In this tutorial, we will learn to use `@todo` tags to document our future tasks, and will view the tasks list from the NetBeans task or action items window:

1. Inside the `TestChild` PHP class or in the preceding document block of the class, we can use a `@todo` tag; inside multiple line comments or DocBlock, add a tag similar to the following:

```
/**
 * @todo have to add class variable and functions
 */
```

In the above document block, we can see that the task has been described beside the tag separated by a whitespace. Also, a `@todo` tag can be added using a single comment line as follows:

```
//TODO need to add class variable and functions
```

2. So, the `TestChild` class may look similar to the following:

```
class TestChild extends Test {

//TODO have to add class variable and functions
}
```

3. As we add the tasks inside the file, the task should be visible in NetBeans' **Tasks** or **Action Items** window; press *Ctrl + 6* to open the window, and the added task should be listed in the **Tasks** window, as shown in the following screenshot:

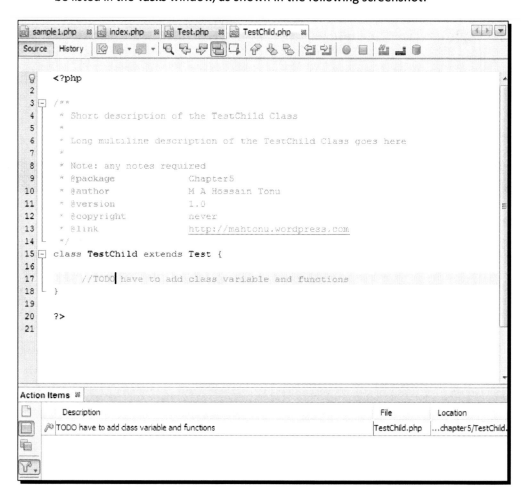

What just happened?

NetBeans updates the task list in the **Task** window as soon as a new task is added using the TODO task marker, and you can have all the tasks listed in that window for the entire project or for all the opened projects at NetBeans. Such tags can be used when we have something in mind that we want to implement and haven't got enough time to write the code, considering its future implementation. So, you can drop the idea in appropriate places using the @todo tag.

So far, we have learned how to use PHPDoc standard tags to document the PHP source elements, and also dealt with DocBlock to write source documentation. Elementary concepts regarding source documentation have been discussed. So, in our next section, we will learn to extract such DocBlocks, to generate HTML documentation for the entire project or API.

Documenting the API

As we have already discussed the significance of source documentation, the documentation should be presented to a general user in a well-organized way or graphically elaborated using HTML pages. Such API documentation, converted from source DocBlocks, can be the technical documentation used for learning about the source. NetBeans comes with the support to generate API documentation from the PHP source for the entire project using the **ApiGen** auto documentor tool.

ApiGen is the tool for creating API documentation using the PHPDoc standard, and supports the latest PHP 5.3 features, such as namespaces, packages, linking between documentation, cross referencing to PHP standard classes and general documentation, creation of highlighted source code, and support for PHP 5.4 traits. It also generates a page with trees of classes, interfaces, traits, and exceptions for the project.

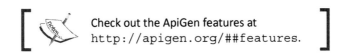

Check out the ApiGen features at
`http://apigen.org/##features`.

In the next section, we will discuss how to install ApiGen and configure it with NetBeans.

Configuring ApiGen

We will first install ApiGen via PEAR and configure it with NetBeans, so that we can generate the API documentation from the IDE. We can automatically install ApiGen and all of its dependencies with PEAR auto-discover enabled. Enabling the discover feature not only automatically adds ApiGen to the system PATH, but also allows for an easy updating of each ApiGen component.

Time for action – installing ApiGen and configuring it with NetBeans

We are already familiar with installing PHP libraries via PEAR (discussed in the previous chapter), and we may have had the PEAR configuration `auto_discover` set to ON. In this section, we will install and configure ApiGen with NetBeans, using the following steps:

1. From the terminal or command prompt, run the following commands to install ApiGen:

```
pear config-set auto_discover 1
pear install pear.apigen.org/apigen
```

The `install` command will automatically download and install ApiGen along with all of its dependencies. Skip the first command if you have already enabled PEAR `auto_discover`.

2. Now, we need to add the ApiGen executable file to the IDE. Open the **IDE Options** window from **Tools | Options**, and choose the **PHP Tab | ApiGen** tab, then click on the **Search...** button to search for ApiGen scripts. The ApiGen scripts should be listed automatically, as shown in the following screenshot:

3. From the previous screenshot, select `apigen.bat` for Windows OS or `apigen` for other OSes, and press **OK** to have the ApiGen script integrated with the IDE, as shown in the following screenshot:

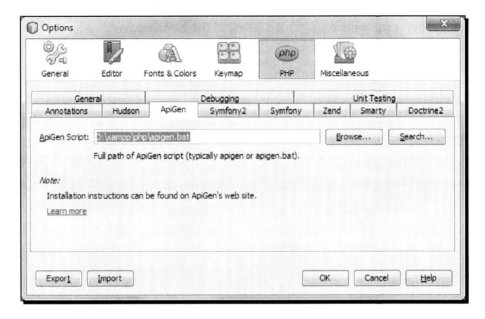

You may browse the ApiGen script path there as well.

4. Press **OK** to save the settings.

What just happened?

Up until now, we have configured the ApiGen tool with NetBeans, and this tool is ready to be used for PHP projects. Once you have integrated the tool with the IDE, you may want to use it from the IDE for the HTML documentation generation for your PHP projects. In our next tutorial, we will learn the usage of the tool from the IDE.

Generating API documentation

We will generate the HTML documentation using ApiGen for the sample PHP project `Chapter5`, and the tool extracts documentation from the DocBlocks available in the project. The generation process can be viewable in the **Output** window of the IDE. Finally, the generated HTML documentation opens in the web browser.

Time for action – generating documentation using ApiGen

Using integrated ApiGen from the IDE, we will run the documentation generator. Note that we need to define the target directory to store the HTML documents. Let's create the HTML documentation for our sample project, according to the following steps:

1. Right-click on the `chapter5` project node. From the context menu, choose **Properties | ApiGen**, and the following **Project Properties** window will be displayed:

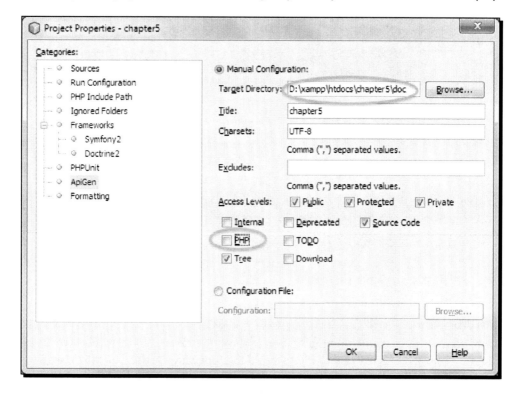

2. From the previous **Project Properties** window, define the **Target Directory** where the HTML pages will be stored, and uncheck the **PHP** box for excluding PHP's default elements from the documentation. In this project, let's create a directory named `doc` as the target directory inside the project, so that the documentation can be browsed at `http://localost/chapter5/doc/`.

3. Click on **OK** to save the settings.

4. Now, right-click on the `chapter5` project node. This will generate a menu, which will look similar to the following screenshot:

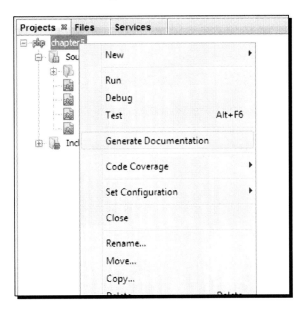

5. From the previous project context menu, choose **Generate Documentation** to start the HTML document generation process, from the given DocBlocks.

6. As soon as we chose **Generate Documentation** in the previous step, the HTML documentation generator started to progress, and completed the HTML documentation. The generation process is summarized in the **Output** window, as follows:

```
Output - Generating API documentation for chapter5
ApiGen 2.6.1
------------
Scanning D:\xampp\htdocs\chapter5
Found 2 classes, 0 constants, 1 functions and other 1 used PHP internal classes
Documentation for 2 classes, 0 constants, 1 functions and other 0 used PHP internal classes will be generated
Using template config file C:\php\pear\data\ApiGen\templates\default\config.neon
Wiping out destination directory
Generating to directory D:\xampp\htdocs\chapter5\doc
Done. Total time: 2 sec, used: 14 MB RAM
```

7. Also the HTML documentation for the entire project has been opened in a browser that looks similar to the following:

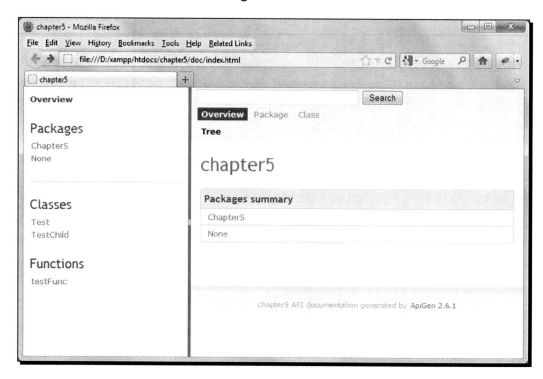

In the above screenshot, we can see that the HTML documentation has been created for the entire project. The documentation is organized according to packages, classes, and functions as per the left frame.

8. Browse through the links created for the project, and explore how the classes and methods are represented over there. You may click on the **TestChild** class link in the previous window to get the following screenshot:

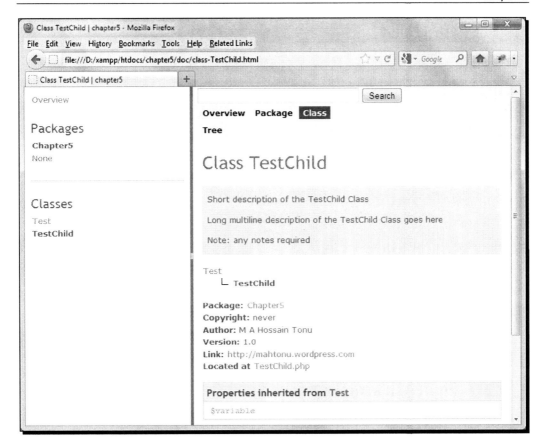

9. In the above screenshot, we can see that the class inheritance is also represented using a tree along with a suitably decorated documentation for the class, as per its DocBlock.

What just happened?

We created a professional API documentation from the source code comments block, and discovered how the classes were organized properly in the final documentation. Note that ApiGen provides a searching facility for classes, functions, and so on at the generated HTML interface, and also provides a customizable template facility to modify the overall documentation's look. We are now confident enough to document the PHP source code effectively.

Pop quiz – reviewing tags

1. Which of the following tags is applicable for only functions or methods?

    a. @author

    b. @package

    c. @param

    d. @link

2. Which of the following tags can be used to document the release version of any element?

    a. @version

    b. @since

    c. @deprecated

    d. @todo

3. Which of the following tags can be used as an inline tag?

    a. @example

    b. @param

    c. @version

    d. @see

Have a go hero – doing more with documentation

Each time you run the NetBeans documentation generator, it wipes out the target directory and creates a new set of HTML documents there. Try commenting interfaces, constants, traits, and so on, and run the documentation generator to test the generated API documents.

Summary

In this chapter, we have discussed and practiced how to document the source code for PHP applications using NetBeans.

We have specially focused on the following topics:

- PHPDoc standards and tags
- Documenting PHP functions/methods, classes, and its variables
- Documenting TODO tasks
- Configuring ApiGen with NetBeans
- API documentation using ApiGen

Finally, it was fun to use the auto-doc generator, and get the HTML documentation generated within a few seconds.

As we are going for the collaborative PHP development in our next chapter, such source documentation is required, in order to maintain a good practice within the development team. In the next chapter, we will learn to use the version control system (Git) from NetBeans.

6
Understanding Git, the NetBeans Way

Commit early and commit often.

In this chapter, we will introduce the version control system, to manage the changes in our source code. To do this, we will learn to use **Git**, a free and open source-distributed version control system. We will use Git from NetBeans in a step-by-step manner. In particular, we will discuss the following issues:

- Version control system
- **Distributed Version Control System (DVCS)**
- Git—the fast and distributed version control system
- Initializing a Git repository
- Cloning a Git repository
- Staging files into a Git repository
- Committing changes to a Git repository
- Comparing file revisions, and reverting changes
- Working with remote repositories—fetching, pulling, and pushing
- Working with branches—creating, checking out, switching, merging, and deleting

Version control system

A version control system (an aspect of **Source Code Management** or **SCM**) is a combination of technologies and practices for tracking and controlling changes to a project's files, particularly for source code, documentation, and web pages.

The reason version control is so universal is that it helps with virtually every aspect of running a project—inter-developer communications, release management, bug management, code stability and experimental development efforts, and attribution and authorization of changes by particular developers. The version control system provides a central coordinating force among all of these areas.

The core activity of version control is **change management**—identifying each discrete change made to the project's files, annotating each change with its metadata, such as the timestamp and author of the change, and then replaying these facts to whoever asks, in whatever way they ask. It is a communications mechanism where a change is the basic unit of information, and such changes can be compared and restored with some types of merged files.

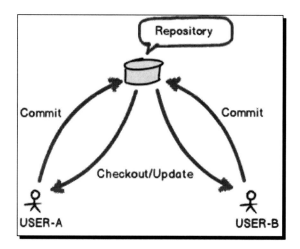

Now let's discuss the common version control system terminologies:

◆ **Repository**: The repository, also known as **repo**, is where the file's current and historical data is stored. At the core of the version control system is the repository, which can have centralized or distributed storage of that system's data. The repository usually stores the information in the form of a filesystem tree, which is a hierarchy of files and directories.

◆ **Working copy**: A working copy is a developer's private directory tree, containing the project's source code files and possibly its web pages, or other documents. A working copy also contains a little bit of metadata managed by the version control system, telling the working copy what repository it comes from, what "revisions" of the files are present, and so on. Generally, each developer has his own working copy, in which he makes and tests the changes, and from which he commits.

In decentralized version control systems, each working copy is a repository in itself, and the changes can be pushed out to (or pulled into) any repository that's willing to accept them.

◆ **Working tree**: This is the tree of actual, checked-out files. The working tree is normally equal to HEAD, plus any local changes that you have made, but not yet committed.

◆ **Origin**: This refers to the original repository, or the default, upstream repository. Most projects have at least one upstream project, which they track. By default, origin is used for this purpose.

◆ **Master**: This refers to the default development branch.

◆ **HEAD**: This is the latest version in a branch.

◆ **Commit**: This is used for making a change to the project; more formally, to store a change in the version control database in such a way that it can be incorporated into the future releases of the project referred to as commit. A commit creates a new version that is essentially a snapshot of the file(s) in your project at a particular point in time.

◆ **Index**: This is a collection of files with stat information, whose contents are stored.

The index is used as a staging area between your working directory and your repository. You can use the index to build up a set of changes that you want to commit together. When you create a commit, what is committed is what is currently in the index, not what is in your working directory.

◆ **Revision**: A "revision" is usually a specific incarnation of one particular file or directory. For example, if the project starts out with revision 6 of file F, and then someone commits a change to F, this produces revision 7 of F.

◆ **Checkout**: Checkout is the process of obtaining a copy of the project, file, revision, and so on from a repository. A checkout usually produces a directory tree called a "working copy", from which changes may be committed back to the original repository.

◆ **Branch**: This is a copy of the project, under version control, but isolated, so that changes made to the branch don't affect the rest of the project. Branches are also known as **lines of development**. Even when a project has no explicit branches, development is still considered to be happening on the "main branch", also known as the "main line" or "trunk".

♦ **Merge**: Merge requires copying a change from one branch to another. This involves merging from the main trunk to some other branch, or vice versa.

Merge has a second related meaning—it is what the version control system does when it sees that two people have changed the same file but in non-overlapping ways. Since the two changes do not interfere with each other, when one person updates their copy of the file (already containing their own changes), the other person's changes will automatically be merged in. This is very common, especially on projects where multiple people are hacking into the same code. When two different changes do overlap, the result is a **conflict**.

♦ **Conflict**: This is what happens when two people try to make different changes to the same area in the code. All version control systems automatically detect conflicts and notify at least one of the humans involved that their changes conflict with someone else's. It is then up to that human to resolve the conflict and communicate that resolution to the version control system.

♦ **Revert**: To roll back to the previous revision, we do revert changes; that is, we throw away the changes and return to the point of the last update. This is handy when you've broken your local build and are unable to figure out how to get it working again. Sometimes reverting is faster than debugging, especially if you have checked in recently.

♦ **Diff**: This is a viewable representation of a change, and it shows which lines were changed and how, plus a few lines of surrounding context on either side. A developer who is already familiar with some code can usually read a diff against that code, understand what the change did, and even spot bugs.

♦ **Tag**: A tag is a label for a particular collection of files at specified revisions. Tags are usually used to preserve interesting snapshots of the project. For example, a tag is usually made for each public release, so that one can obtain, directly from the version control system, the exact set of files/revisions comprising that release.

Distributed version control

Some version control systems are centralized—there is a single master repository, which stores all the changes made to the project. Others are decentralized—each developer has their own repository, and changes can be swapped back and forth between repositories, arbitrarily.

In distributed version control systems (such as Git, Mercurial, or Bazaar), developers (clients) don't just check out the latest snapshot of the files, but also fully mirror the repository.

Lets have look at the distributed version control schematic diagram:

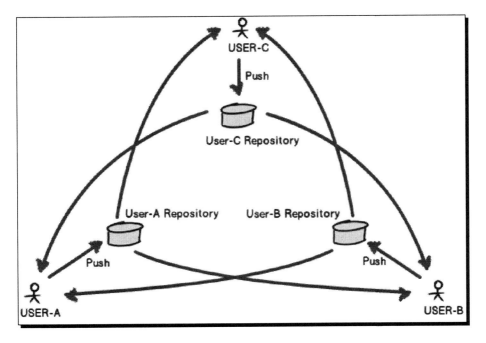

Git – the fast and distributed version control system

Git is a free and open source distributed version control system, designed to handle everything from small to very large projects with speed and efficiency. In Git, you can have your own local repository and nearly all the operations in local.

Every Git clone is a fully-fledged repository with a complete history and full revision-tracking capabilities, which are not dependent on network access or a central server. Branching and merging are fast and easy to do.

Git is used for the version control of files, much like tools such as Mercurial, Subversion, CVS, Perforce (`http://git-scm.com/`).

 Git was initially designed and developed by *Linus Torvalds* for Linux kernel development.

Understanding Git, the NetBeans way

The NetBeans IDE provides excellent support for the Git version control client. The IDE's Git support allows you to perform versioning tasks directly from your project within the IDE. You can have the Git repository in two approaches, where the first one takes an existing project or directory and imports it into Git, and the second one clones an existing Git repository from another server computer.

In our upcoming sections, using NetBeans, we will try to initiate a Git repository and learn how to clone a Git repository. To do this, we will create a sample NetBeans project named Chapter6 with the project metadata stored in a separate directory, as we don't need the project metadata under version control, and will practice in the project directory.

Initializing a Git repository

If you are starting to track an existing project in Git, or want your existing project under version control, then you want to initiate the Git repository.

Time for action – initializing a Git repository

To initialize a Git repository from your existing project or source files, which are not under version control yet, you can go through the following steps:

1. Right-click on the project Chapter6, and select **Versioning | Initialize Git Repository** from the context menu.

2. Now, specify the directory path where the repository will be created in the **Initialize a Git Repository** dialog box. In our case, we choose the same project path.

3. Click on **OK** and you can check the repository creation progress or status in the **Output** window (*Ctrl+4*) as follows:

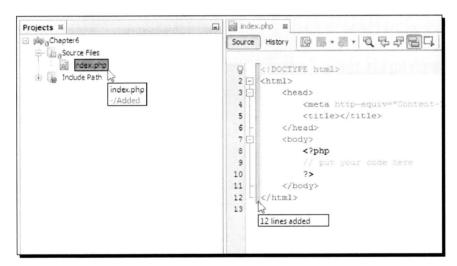

A `.git` subdirectory will be created under your project directory, where all the data of your project snapshots is stored. Git starts versioning all the files in the specified directory.

You can see that all the project file(s) are marked as `-/Added` in the project tree. To view a file status, just hover on the filename, as shown in the following screenshot:

We can see that the file status has been displayed in green, to the right of the slash.

Also note that the newly added lines inside the `index.php` file are marked with green, as shown in the previous screenshot. You can see the number of added lines since the earlier version, hovering on the green highlights. As soon as the Git repository is created, all the options for Git from the IDE can be available directly under the **Team** menu or the **Team | Git** submenu for the current project.

What just happened?

We have successfully initialized the Git repository for placing our existing project files under version control using NetBeans. Thus, we have our own fully-fledged local Git repository.

To work with remote repositories, you may add a remote Git repository as the origin of this initialized repo. In this way, you can perform a remote repository syncing with your local repository. Now, we can add files or directly commit them to the local Git repository; but before that, let's try the second approach with cloning a Git repository. Note that along with cloning a repository, we may also create another new project.

Cloning a Git repository

Say you have been added as a collaborator into an existing project maintained under Git. If you want to get a copy of an existing Git repository or a project you would like to contribute to, you will need a Git clone of that repo for it. A direct collaborator is a trusted and experienced developer added by the repository owner, who contributes to the project and can perform regular Git operations into the original repository.

For this tutorial, we have already created a Git repository at GitHub.com (free Git hosting) named `chapter6demo` (`https://github.com/mahtonu/chapter6demo`), and for test purposes, we have added another account as a collaborator over there. Now, we are going to clone that repository from GitHub.com and practice regular Git features from the NetBeans IDE using that collaborator account. To clone via SSH and to perform as a collaborator on a GitHub project, you need a GitHub account, and need to be added as a member into the project by the corresponding project owner.

> To host your source code at GitHub.com, sign up and create your own repository over there.
>
> Also, you need to add your public key at **Settings | SSH keys** (`https://github.com/settings/ssh`) for Git operations via **Secure Shell (SSH)**, from your computer.
>
> For Windows OS, you may use **PuTTYgen** (`http://www.chiark.greenend.org.uk/~sgtatham/putty/download.html`) to generate your keys, and must convert them into the **OpenSSH** format before using them in the IDE.

Before proceeding with the following tutorial, you may create a sample repository at GitHub and add another GitHub test account as collaborator into the repository (from **ADMIN | Collaborators**), and remember to add Public keys for those corresponding accounts.

Time for action – cloning a Git repository from GitHub via the SSH protocol

For this tutorial, we will act as a collaborator to that GitHub project, and have our own SSH public key added to the GitHub account. We will add our SSH private key using NetBeans. Along with repository cloning, NetBeans provides the option to create a fresh new project:

1. Select **Team | Git | Clone…**, and the **Clone Repository** wizard will be displayed.

2. Specify the path to the repository required in the **Repository URL** field, for example git@github.com:mahtonu/chapter6demo.git.

3. Verify that **Username** is git.

4. Browse the **Private Key File** location.

5. Add **Passphrase**, which you created during the key generation, and (optionally) select the **Save Passphrase** checkbox. The **Remote Repository** page at the **Clone Repository** wizard looks similar to the following screenshot:

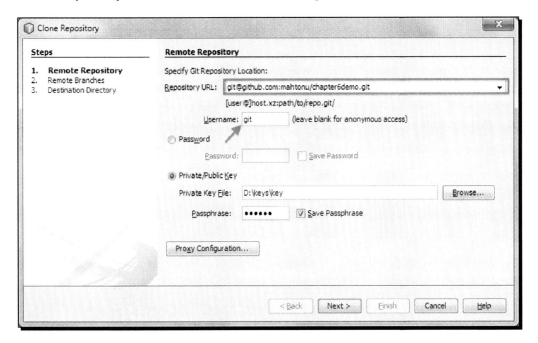

6. Click on **Next**, and select the repository branch that needs to be fetched (downloaded) to your local repository at the **Remote Branches** page, for example, `master`.

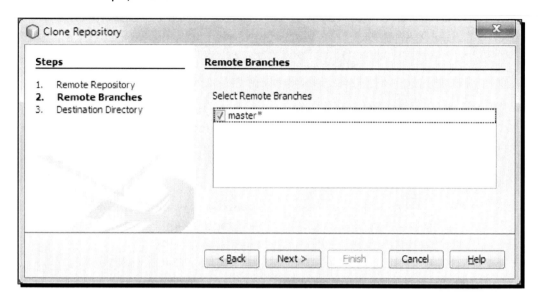

7. Click on **Next**, and fill in or browse the **Parent Directory** where the clone directory will be placed at the **Destination Directory** page. The repository name is filled in the **Clone Name** field automatically, which will be the local clone directory name.

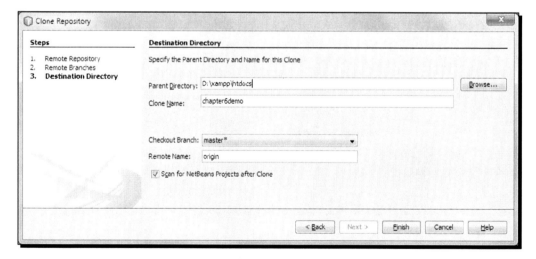

8. In this screenshot, **Checkout Branch** is set to `master*` by default, and **Remote Name** is set to `origin`, which means that it is the original repository that we are going to clone. Also, leave the **Scan for NetBeans Projects after Clone** checkbox checked.

9. Click on **Finish** and see what is happening in the NetBeans **Output** window. You will be prompted to create a new NetBeans project from the cloned source, as shown in the following screenshot:

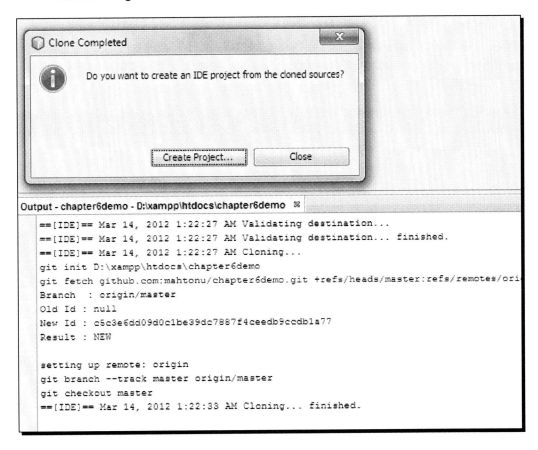

We created the NetBeans project from the cloned source as well, by selecting **New Project** with the existing sources option and storing the NetBeans project metadata into a separate directory, as we don't want them to be under Git. Also, you will find a single README file inside the project, which is already tracked and comes from the remote origin repository.

What just happened?

We have cloned a repository via the SSH protocol, using NetBeans. Each of these clones acts as a fully-fledged repo, and a `.git` directory inside them contains all the revision information. So, now we have a working local repository and can work with the remote origin as well. What we have done is added one of our GitHub accounts into a GitHub project as the collaborator, and as we got access to that project, we cloned it from there using the NetBeans IDE. You can perform most Git operations from the IDE, and the results of these operations can be seen in the **Output** window.

From this point, we will learn to use Git operations from the IDE. The next sections are illustrated from a collaborator's perspective of adding, editing, comparing, committing files, pushing changes to remote, and so on.

Pop quiz – understanding Git

1. Which is the correct feature of Git?

    a. Distributed version control system

    b. Issue tracker

    c. Centralized repository

    d. Always network dependent

2. Which is not a Git repository feature?

    a. Each Git clone is a fully-fledged repository

    b. A local Git repository is the subset of the original repository

    c. All the commits are local

    d. May have a remote origin

3. In our preceding section, which key file was added into the IDE?

    a. Public Key file

    b. Private Key file

    c. Both the key files

    d. Open SSH file

4. What will be the file status symbol in the context of a repository in the NetBeans IDE for a newly created file?

    a. `Added/-`

    b. `-/Added`

    c. `Added/+`

    d. `+/Added`

Staging files to a Git repository

To start tracking a new file and also to stage changes to an already tracked file in the Git repository, you want to add it to the repository. **Staging** means adding new or modified files under Git for "*changes to be committed*".

When adding files to a Git repository, the IDE first composes and saves snapshots of your project in the **Index**. After you perform the commit, the IDE saves these snapshots in the HEAD.

Time for action – staging files to a Git repository

In this tutorial, we will learn how to stage files to our local Git repository. Staging is the state to add the changes to be committed. The following files can be called staged files:

♦ A newly created file added to the repository

♦ An existing file modified and added to the repository

First, we will add a newly created file to the repo, and then we will add a modified file to repo:

1. First of all, we will open the **Show Changes** viewer window of NetBeans Git. Right-click on the `chapter6demo` project node, and select **Git | Show Changes**. NetBeans will scan the repository and show any changes in the window. Now, any changes into the repository can be viewable in real time from this window.

2. Now, add a new file into the NetBeans project in the usual way, which is `test.php`. You can see that the new `test.php` file is opened into the editor; hovering on the filename at the **Projects** pane shows the file status for Git.

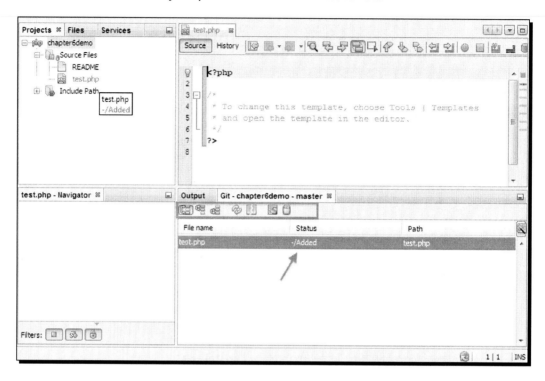

In this screenshot, we can see that the bottom of the Git window shows `test.php` as the newly added file, denoted as `-/Added`, which means that it's not added to the repo yet.

3. Right-click on `test.php`, and select **Git | Add** from the context menu. Now, the `test.php` file is available or can be tracked under Git. You can see the file status at the Git window as `Added/-`, which means that the file is ready to be committed or has been staged. Also, you can see the output window showing the Git operation status as well.

4. Now, we will open the existing README file, try to add some lines within it, and save it, to watch the effect it has in the local repository. Note that the file comes from the original remote repository. We can also view any changes in the Git window instantly.

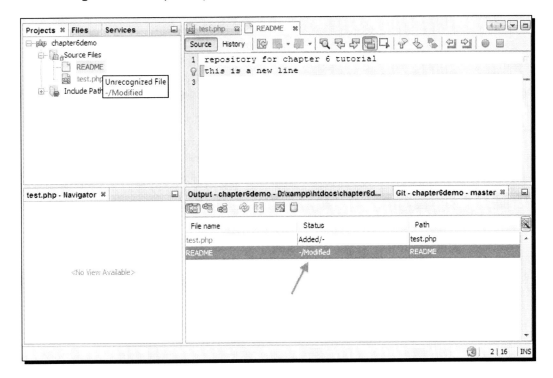

In this screenshot, we can see that a new line added to the file (marked in green) at the beginning states that the new line has been added from the earlier version. Also, at the Git window, you can see that the file status shows as -/Modified, which means the file has been modified but not added for staging yet.

5. Right-click on **README**, and select **Git | Add** from the context menu. Now, the README file changes have been staged for commit. You can see the file status in the Git window as Modified/-, which means the file is either ready to be committed or has been staged. Note that each time you finish the modification of the file, you can repeat the step to stage the changes for the next commit. Also, the modified filename becomes blue, and the newly added filename becomes green within the NetBeans **Projects** pane.

What just happened?

We just learned how to stage files for the changes done so far, which are to be committed in the local repository. So, each time we have some changes, we may apply **Git | Add** to those files, in order to make them available for the next commit. Also, we have seen that the Git window shows the real-time status of the files in contrast to that of the repository.

Note that the **Team** menu contains all the options immediately under it for that particular versioning system in use for the active project. For example, in our case, we can see that all the Git options are available under both the **Team** menu and the **Team | Git** submenu.

Viewing changes in the source editor

When you have a versioned file open in the IDE's source editor, you can view real-time changes occurring to your file as you modify it against the base version from the Git repository. As you work, the IDE uses color codes in the source editor's margins to convey the following information:

- ◆ Blue: Indicates lines that have been changed since the earlier revision
- ◆ Green: Indicates lines that have been added since the earlier revision
- ◆ Red: Indicates lines that have been removed since the earlier revision

The source editor's left margin shows changes occurring on a line-by-line basis. When you modify a given line, changes are immediately shown in the left margin.

The source editor's right margin provides you with an overview, which displays changes made to your file as a whole, from top to bottom. Color coding is immediately generated when you make changes to your file. You can click on a specific point within the right margin to bring your inline cursor immediately to that location in the file.

Git window

You have already seen a real-time list of all of the changes made to the files within a selected folder of your local working tree in the Git window, as shown in the following screenshot:

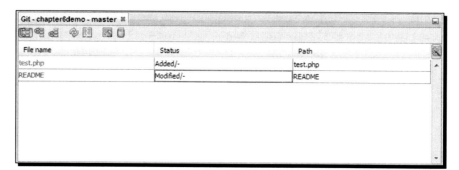

In this versioning window, you can see a toolbar with buttons, which enables you to invoke the most common Git tasks on all files displayed in the list. Using the buttons in the toolbar, you can choose to display the list of files that have differences in either the Index or the HEAD, the working tree and the Index, or the working tree and the HEAD. You can also click on the column headings above the listed files, to sort the files by name, status, or location.

Have a go hero – unstaging a staged file

Let's say that you have changed two files and want to commit them as two separate changes, but unintentionally staged them both. Try to unstage a staged file using **Team | Git | Reset...**; you may reset the HEAD from there.

Committing changes to the repository

In this section, we will learn how to commit changes that have been staged. The changes made in the previous section will be committed into the local repository.

Time for action – committing changes to the local repository

To commit changes to the local repository, go through the following steps:

1. Select the file you want to commit to your local repository; that is `test.php`. Right-click on them and select **Git | Commit...** from the context menu. The commit dialog box will be displayed, as shown in the following screenshot:

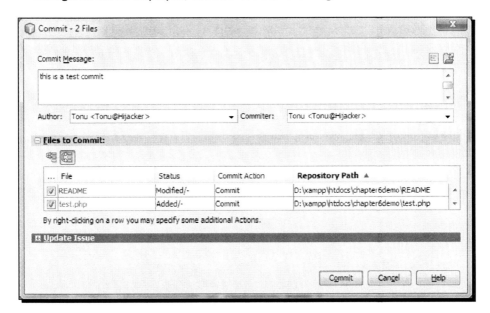

In this screenshot, you can see the **Commit Message** box. The **Files to Commit** list shows the staged files to be committed.

2. Type in a message for the **Commit Message** text area that will describe the intent of your source code commit. The commit message should convey a meaningful description of what the changes are and why.

3. You can exclude a file from commit by unchecking the row, or you may specify some additional actions by right-clicking on a row. Click on **Commit** when you are done.

What just happened?

The IDE executed the commit and stored your snapshots to the repository. The IDE's status bar, located at the bottom-right of the interface, was displayed as the commit action took place. Upon a successful commit, versioning badges disappear in the **Projects**, **Files**, and **Favorites** windows, and the color code of committed files returns to normal. Also note that files at the **Git** window cleared, which means that the repository is up-to-date and no changes are available.

Have a go hero – adding and committing all the files together

We have staged new files to the repository and then committed those changes. Now, directly commit the new files to have them automatically staged from the IDE. You may add new files to the project; try to commit them directly, and see the difference.

Comparing file revisions

Comparing file versions is a common job when working with versioned projects. The IDE enables you to compare revisions by using the `Diff` command. File revisions can be compared to see the source changes from one revision to another.

Time for action – using diff from the IDE

In order to compare the file revisions, you can use the `Diff` feature of the IDE and go through the following steps:

1. Select a versioned file that is `README`, and modify some lines of the file.

2. Right-click on the file, and select **Git | Diff** from the context menu. A graphical **Diff** viewer is opened for all the selected file(s) and revisions in the IDE's main window. The **Diff** viewer displays two copies in side-by-side panels. The more current copy appears on the right side. So if you are comparing a repository revision against your working tree, the working tree gets displayed in the right panel:

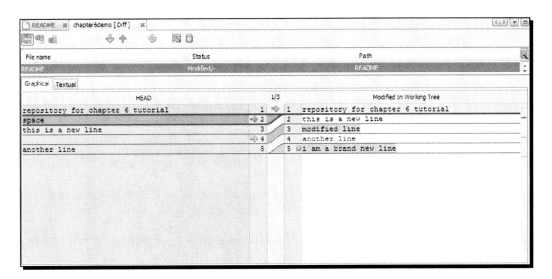

The Diff viewer makes use of the same color codes used elsewhere, to display version control changes. In the previous screenshot, the green block indicates the content that has been added to the more current revision. The red block indicates that the content from the earlier revision has been removed. The blue block indicates that changes have occurred within the highlighted line(s).

What just happened?

The **Diff** viewer toolbar also includes buttons that enable you to invoke the most common Git tasks for all the files displayed in the list. If you are performing a diff on your local copy in the working tree, the editor enables you to make changes directly from within the **Diff** viewer. To do so, you can place your cursor within the right pane of the **Diff** viewer and modify your file accordingly. Otherwise, make use of the inline icons, which display adjacent to each highlighted change.

Reverting the local changes of the repository

Reverting is required for throwing away the local changes made to selected files in your working tree, and replacing these files with the ones in the Index or HEAD.

Time for action – reverting changes of the working tree

To revert the changes, go through the following steps:

1. From the previous section, the **Diff** window of the modified README file provides a reverting, modification facility. Also, the Git window provides buttons for reverting modifications.

2. Right-click on the README file, and select **Git | Revert | Revert Modifications** from the context menu, or click on the **Revert Modifications** button from the **Diff** window. A dialog box similar to the following one opens:

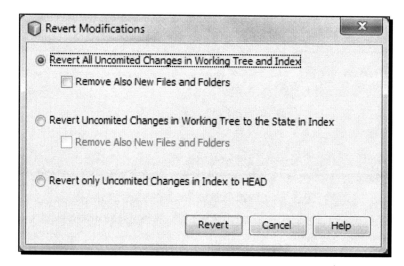

3. Specify additional options (for example **Revert only Uncomited Changes in Index to HEAD**).

4. Click on **Revert**.

What just happened?

The IDE reverted the changes specified and replaced those files with the ones in the Index or HEAD. In this way, you can easily revert the modifications or revert commits as well.

Pop quiz – working with Git

1. When adding files to a Git repository, the IDE first composes and saves snapshots of your project in which of the following?

    a. Index

    b. HEAD

    c. Repository

    d. Master

2. Which color in the source editor's left margin indicates lines that have been changed since the earlier revision?

    a. Green

    b. Blue

    c. Red

    d. Yellow

3. Diff is used for which of the following?

    a. To view file history

    b. To compare two revisions

    c. To compare two revisions of two files

    d. All of the above

4. What can be done with revert in case of reverting changes?

    a. Revert all uncommitted changes in the working tree and Index

    b. Revert uncommitted changes in the working tree, to the state in Index

    c. Revert only uncommitted changes to HEAD in the Index

    d. All of the above

Have a go hero – reverting commits

Try to revert specific commits from the IDE using the commit ID. To do so, you may select **Revert | Revert Commit...** from the IDE.

Working with remote repositories

To work with other developers or in a collaborative, development environment, everyone wants to share their work, which involves fetching, pushing, and pulling data to and from remote repositories hosted on the Internet or network.

Fetching source code updates

Fetching gets the changes from the original remote repository that you do not have yet. It doesn't change any of your local branches. Fetching gets all the branches from the remote repositories, which you can merge into your branch or just inspect at any time.

Time for action – fetching source code updates

To fetch the updates, go through the following steps:

1. Right-click on the project node, select **Git | Remote | Fetch**, and the **Fetch from Remote Repository** wizard is displayed.

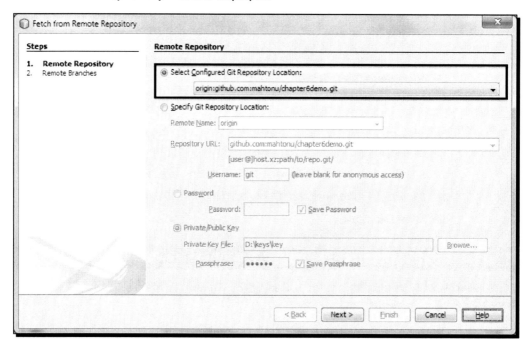

2. At the **Remote Repository** page of the wizard, we will use the configured repository (to use the path to the repository configured earlier) and click on **Next**.

3. At the **Remote Branches** page of the wizard, select the branches to fetch changes from, and click on **Finish**. Find the local copy of a remote branch in the repository browser window (**TEAM | Git | Repository Browser**).

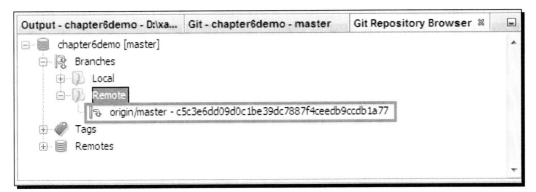

What just happened?

A local copy of a remote branch was created. The selected branches are updated in the **Branches | Remote** directory in **Git Repository Browser**. Next, the fetched updates are merged into a local branch.

Pulling updates from the remote repository

When pulling some updates from a remote Git repository, the changes are fetched from it and merged into the current HEAD for your local repository.

Time for action – pulling updates from the remote repository

To perform pulling, complete the following steps:

1. Right-click on the project node, select **Git | Remote | Pull**, and the **Pull from Remote Repository** wizard is displayed.

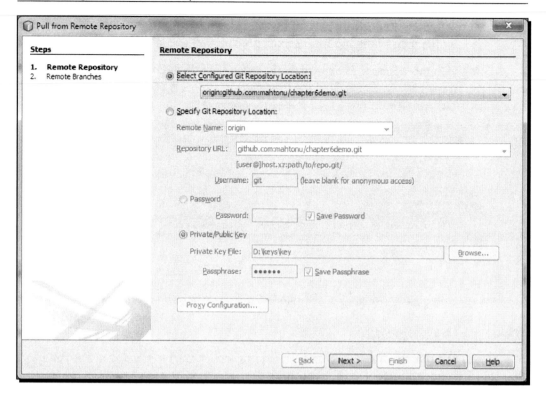

2. At the **Remote Repository** page of the wizard, we will use the configured repository (to use the path to the repository configured earlier), and click on **Next**.

3. At the **Remote Branches** page of the wizard, select the branch, that is `master ->` `origin/master` (remote branch `origin/master` will be merged into the current branch), to pull the changes, and click on **Finish**.

What just happened?

Your local repository is synchronized with the origin repository. At the **Remote Branches** page, the branches we choose, that is `master -> origin/master`, will be merged into our current branch. You can see the pulling status at the bottom right of the IDE or in the output window as well.

In the simplest terms, `Git Pull` does a `Git Fetch` followed by a `Git Merge`.

Pushing source code changes to a remote repository

To share the cool commits you've done so far, you want to push your changes to the remote repository. Again, you can push your new branches and data to the remote repository.

Time for action – pushing source code changes

To contribute changes from your local Git repository into a public/remote Git repository, perform the following steps:

1. Right-click on project node, select **Git | Remote | Push**, and the **Push to Remote Repository** wizard is displayed.

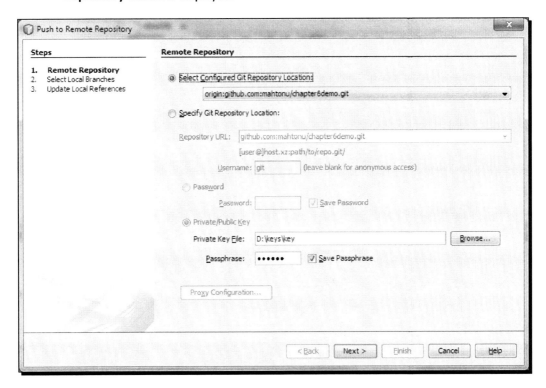

2. At the **Remote Repository** page of the wizard, we will use the configured repository (to use the path to the repository configured earlier), and click on **Next**.

3. At the **Select Local Branches** page of the wizard, select the local branches, that is `master -> master`, to push your changes to, and click on **Finish**.

4. At the **Update Local References** page, select the branch (es), that is `master -> origin/master`, to be updated in the **Remotes** directory of your local repository, and click on **Finish**.

What just happened?

The specified remote repository branch was updated with the latest state of your local branch. Your local repo's **Branches | Remote** directory was updated as well. So, your changes are live at the remote repository, and other collaborators can pull the changes to their own repos.

Working with branches

The intent to start an alternative line of development generates a branch in the source code management system. **Branch** helps you to manage working contexts and provide separate workspaces. Generally, **Master Branch** is the one where the finest piece of code resides; along with it, there could be a **Development Branch** where the continuous development code can reside. Again, sensible software development uses branches to maintain features, releases, hotfixes, and so on.

For the development of a new version and maintenance of an old version, branching is a definite. In the following diagram, a generic Git branching model is described:

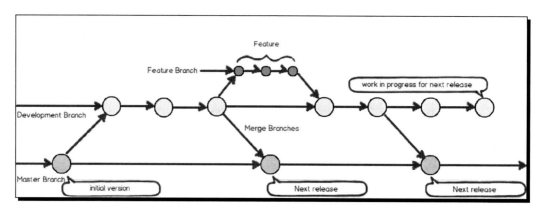

In this diagram, we can see that **Development Branch** merged with **Master Branch** for a new release, and a new feature has been merged with **Development Branch**.

NetBeans supports you to do the following things with Git Branches:

- Creating a branch
- Checking out a branch
- Switching branches
- Merging branches
- Deleting branches

Creating a branch

If you want to work on a separate version of your file system for stabilization or experimentation purposes without disturbing the main trunk, you can create a branch.

Time for action – creating a branch

To create a local branch, complete the following steps:

1. Right-click on the project node, select **Git | Branch | Create Branch**, and the **Create Branch** dialog box is displayed.

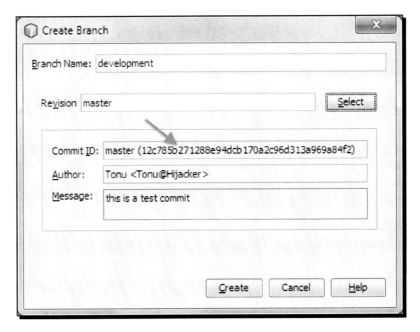

2. In the **Branch Name** field, type in the desired branch name to be created, which is `development`.

3. You may type a specific revision of the selected item by entering a commit ID, existing branch, or tag name in the **Revision** field, or press **Select** to view the list of revisions maintained in the repository. The default **Revision** is the latest revision from the master branch.

4. Optionally, in the **Select Revision** dialog box, expand **Branches** and select the branch required, specify the commit ID in the adjacent list, and press **Select**.

5. Review the **Commit ID**, **Author**, and **Message** fields information, specific to the revision being branched from, and click on **Create**. The branch is added to the **Branches | Local** folder of the Git repository view at **Git Repository Browser**.

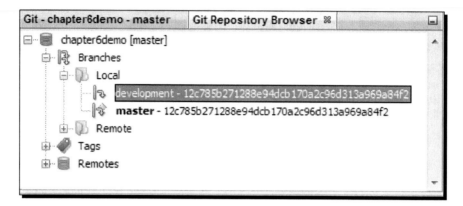

What just happened?

We have created a new branch in our local repository. The new branch contains the latest snapshot from the master branch. The newly created branch is not our working branch yet. The master branch is still the working branch; we'll choose to check out the new branch to make it a working one. Note that we can create new branches from any existing revisions.

Checking out a branch

If you want to edit files on a branch that already exists, you can check out the branch that needs to be used to copy the files to your working tree. It will simply make a switch to the desired branch.

Time for action – checking out a branch

To check out a revision, perform the following:

1. Right-click on the project node, select **Git | Checkout | Checkout Revision**, and the **Checkout Revision** dialog box is displayed.

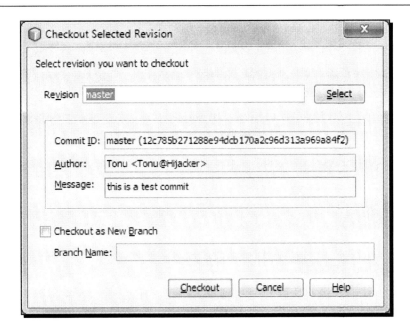

2. Again, right-click on the **Branches | Local | Branch Name** at the **Repository Browser** window from the context menu, as shown in the following screenshot. Select **Checkout Revision**, and the same dialog box is displayed, along with the latest revision selected from that branch.

3. Optionally, specify the revision required, by entering a commit ID, existing branch, or tag name in the **Revision** field, or press **Select** to view the list of revisions maintained in the repository. Note that if the specified revision refers to a valid commit that is not marked with a branch name, then your HEAD becomes detached and you are no longer on any branch.

4. Optionally, in the **Select Revision** dialog box, expand **Branches** and select the branch required, specify the commit ID in the adjacent list, and press **Select**.

5. Review the **Commit ID**, **Author**, and **Message** fields information specific to the revision being checked out.

6. To create a new branch out of the checked out revision, select the **Checkout as New Branch** option, and enter the name in the **Branch Name** field.

7. Press **Checkout** to check out the revision.

What just happened?

Files in the working tree and Index were updated to match the version in the specified revision.

Switching to a branch

If you want to switch your files to a branch that already exists (for example, to a commit that is not at the top of one of your branches), you can use the **Team | Git | Branch | Switch To Branch** command, specify the branch in the **Switch to Selected Branch** dialog box, check it out as a new branch (optionally), and press **Switch**.

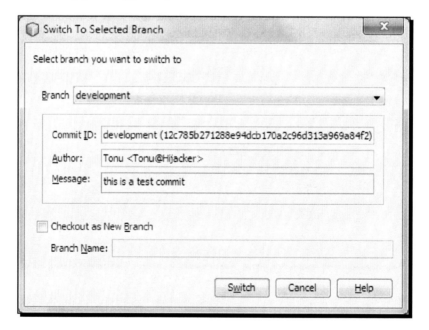

Checking out files

The IDE supports context-sensitive checkout of the file(s), folder(s), or project(s) currently selected in the IDE. To check out some files (not a branch) from the Index, select **Team | Git | Checkout | Checkout Files** from the main menu, and the **Checkout Selected Paths** dialog box is displayed.

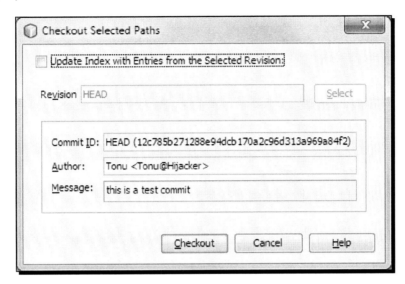

From this dialog box, select **Update Index with Entries** from the **Selected Revision** option. If selected, the Index is updated with the state in the selected revision prior to the checkout itself (that is, the selected files in both the working tree and Index are updated).

Specify the required attributes and check out.

Merging

Merge a branch context into your current one. Once you have work isolated in a branch, you will eventually want to incorporate it into your main branch. You can merge any branch into your current branch.

Time for action – merging into current branch

To port the modifications from a repository revision to the working tree, do the following:

1. Select **Team | Git | Merge Revision** from the main menu. The **Merge Revision** dialog box is displayed.

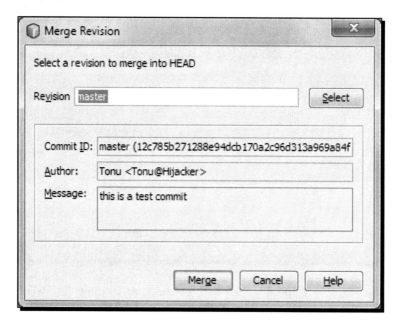

2. (Optional) Specify the revision required by entering a commit ID, existing branch, or tag name in the **Revision** field, or press **Select** to view the list of revisions maintained in the repository.

3. (Optional) In the **Select Revision** dialog box, expand **Branches** and select the branch required, specify the commit ID in the adjacent list, and press **Select**.

4. Review the **Commit ID**, **Author**, and **Message** fields information specific to the revision being merged.

5. Press **Merge**.

What just happened?

A three-way merge among the current branches, your working tree content, and the specified branch is done. If a merge conflict occurs, the conflicting file is marked with a red badge to indicate this. After merging, you can still commit the changes, in order for them to be added to the HEAD.

Deleting a branch

To delete an unnecessary local branch, select **Team | Git | Repository Browser** from the main menu. In **Git Repository Browser**, select the branch that needs to be deleted. Note that the branch is supposed to be inactive, which means it has not been currently checked out in the working tree.

Right-click the selected branch, and select **Delete Branch** from the pop-up menu. In the **Delete Branch** dialog box, press **OK** to confirm the branch deletion. The branch is removed from the local repository, as well as from **Git Repository Browser**.

Pop quiz – working with remote repositories and branches

1. Which Git operations can be the most relevant for remote repositories?

    a. Committing, merging, and reverting

    b. Fetching, pulling, and pushing

    c. Fetching, pulling, pushing, and checking out

    d. Adding, committing, and pushing

2. What happens after you pull changes from a remote repository?

    a. Changes are fetched from the remote repository

    b. Changes are fetched from it and merged into the current HEAD of your local repository

    c. Changes are fetched from it and merged into the current HEAD of your remote repository

    d. None of the above

3. What happens after checking out a branch?

    a. It switches to that branch immediately, and the branch files become available to your working tree

    b. It copies the files to your working tree

    c. A new branch is created, and it becomes your working branch

    d. All of the above

Have a go hero – creating tags

Git uses two main types of tags—**lightweight** and **annotated**. A lightweight tag is very much like a branch that doesn't change— it's just a pointer to a specific commit. Annotated tags, however, are stored as full objects in the Git database. Such tags check the sum and contain the tagger's name, e-mail, and date along with a tagging message. It's generally recommended that you create annotated tags so you can have all this information. Now, create a new tag, and you may select **Git | Tag | Create Tag...** from the IDE.

Good practices and workflow

A few guidelines and workflows are discussed below, in order to uphold good practice with Git:

- Always maintain a separate branch for whatever thing you're doing. Now, when you would like to merge your changes back into main, simply do a Git Merge.
- Keep your branch up-to-date, if possible, which involves checking out or pulling changes.
- Branches can be pushed up to the origin. There are a few reasons for this. First, if your workstation crashes, you don't lose your changes—one of the primary reasons for a VCS. Second, other developers can quickly switch to your branch if needed.
- Commit your changes often; of course, one should always commit changes in logical pieces. Since your changes are committed locally, not to the origin/master server (can be done with a push), you should commit changes in an organized way.
- Provide a message/comment for everything you do with the commit message and for every operation that makes a change to the revision history.
- Push your changes often. If you're developing in your own branch that's separate from everyone else, your changes will not affect anyone else.

Preferred Git workflow:

- Create a branch from the master node, check it out, and do your work
- Test and commit your changes
- Optionally, push your branch up to the remote repository (origin)
- Check out master, make sure it's up-to-date with upstream changes
- Merge your branch into master
- Test again (and again)
- Push your local copy of master up to the remote repository master (origin/master)
- Delete your branch (and remotely too, if you published it)

Moreover, using the version control system can be worth it even for a local standalone project, because the code changes can be easily reviewed, rolled back, and backed up locally.

Summary

In this chapter, we've discussed the version control system and why it is so important. Also, we have picked Git as a distributed version control system, and learned how to use it from NetBeans.

We have especially focused on the following:

- Distributed Version Control System or DVCS
- Initializing a Git repository
- Cloning a Git repository
- Staging files into a Git repository
- Committing changes to a Git Repository
- Comparing file revisions and reverting changes
- Working with remote repositories—fetching, pulling, and pushing
- Working with branches—creating, checking out, switching, merging, and deleting.

Finally, we have discussed the practices and the preferred workflow for Git. We are now much more confident to join a collaborative development using Git and NetBeans.

In the next chapter, we will create a new PHP project with a user registration, login, and logout, to advance our PHP application development skills to the next level.

7

Building User Registration, Login, and Logout

Always plan ahead. It wasn't raining when Noah built the ark
- Richard C. Cushing.

From this chapter onwards, we will get our hands dirty with professional PHP projects. We will design and develop a web applicaton where users can register themselves, and after registraton they can login to the applicaton, view, and update their own profle, and so on.

In this chapter, we will work out the following topics:

- ◆ Application architecture
- ◆ Designing the API
- ◆ User registration
- ◆ User login and logout
- ◆ User profile view and update

Planning the project

Project planning is always signified as planning for the future, which means that a project should be planned, as it can be extended easily or can be reusable, more modular, and even scalable. For this project, we will design the application architecture in a realistic manner, so the user registration, login, and logout application can also be easily used in our future projects.

We will design the **Application Programming Interface (API)** and build the application using that API. The API will facilitate the application for any sort of user signup or signin related tasks, so that the core of the project is the API. Once we have the API ready, we can easily build a number of applications using that API.

First of all, let's think about the API design. Remember that we will use some architectural pattern, that is the **Data Access Object (DAO)** pattern for our projects.

 It is strongly recommended for this project to have prior knowledge of **Object Oriented Programming (OOP)** concepts.

Understanding the application architecture

The architecture needs to be built up in layers in data storage, data access, application services, and the application. This is depicted in the following screenshot:

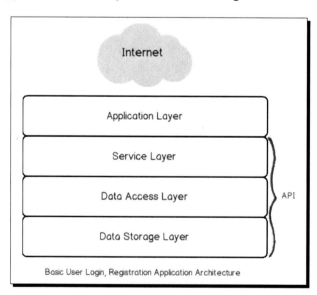

Basic User Login, Registration Application Architecture

Each layer can be designated as a group of analogous logical tasks, as the data storage layer acts as a data source, such as a relational database, a filesystem, or any other data source. The **data access layer** communicates with the data source to get or store data from the **storage layer**, and provides a nice abstraction in the data source to be delivered to the **service layer**. The service layer is a medium of data persistence with the **application layer**, and also offers other services, such as a validation service. The **data access objects** reside in the data access layer, and the **business objects** reside in the **service layer**. Finally, the **applications** reside in the application layer, which directly deals with end users. So, the service layer could be the surface tier for our API, in such a layered design.

Now, let's consider particular functionalities, such as registration, login, validation, and data abstraction into each unit or module. So, each layer will have compulsory units, as shown in the following diagram:

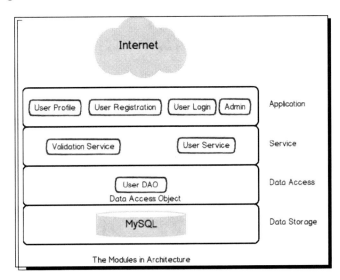

We can easily understand that each layer contains its appropriate modules. For example, the DAO module resides in the data access layer, the service layer has its service units such as Validation, and the user service module and application layer contain user login, user registration, user profile, and admin modules. For our project to grasp the architectural concepts quickly, we will try to keep each module as a simple PHP class with associated codes.

So, let's have a quick look at what we will be building finally.

The following screenshot represents the **User Registration** screen with **Name**, **Email**, **Password**, and **Phone** fields:

The following screenshot represents the **User Login** screen with the **Remember me next time** option:

The following screenshot represents the **User Profile** view with the **Logout** and **Edit Account** menus at the top:

Understanding the DAO pattern

The DAO is used to abstract and encapsulate all access to the data source. The DAO manages the connection with the data source, to obtain and store the data.

> *"The DAO implements the access mechanism required to work with the data source. The data source could be a persistent store like an RDBMS, an external service like a B2B exchange, a repository like an LDAP database, or a business service or low-level sockets. The business component that relies on the DAO uses the simpler interface exposed by the DAO for its clients.*
>
> *The DAO completely hides the data source implementation details from its clients (data client). Because the interface exposed by the DAO to clients does not change when the underlying data source implementation changes, this pattern allows the DAO to adapt to different storage schemes without affecting its clients or business components. Essentially, the DAO acts as an adapter between the component and the data source. The pattern originates from the core J2EE pattern."*

```
http://java.sun.com/blueprints/corej2eepatterns/Patterns/
DataAccessObject.html.
```

The purpose of using DAO is relatively simple, as follows:

- It can be used in a large percentage of applications, wherever data storage is required
- It hides all the details of the data storage from the rest of the application
- It acts as an intermediary between your application and the database
- It allows ripple effects from the possible changes to the persistence mechanism to be confined to a specific area

Reviewing OOP issues

Let's have a look at a few object-oriented programming keywords for access modifiers or properties:

- `Public`: This property or method can be used from anywhere in the script.
- `Private`: This property or method can be used only by the class or object it is part of; it cannot be accessed elsewhere.
- `Protected`: This property or method can be used only by code in the class it is part of, or by children of that class.
- `Final`: This method, or class, cannot be overridden in subclasses.
- `Abstract`: This method or class cannot be used directly, and you have to subclass this; it cannot be instantiated.

- ◆ `Static`: This property or method belongs to the class itself and not to any instance of it. You can also think of static properties as global variables that sit inside a class, but are accessible from anywhere via the class. Static members can be accessed using the `::` operator after the class name.

Namespace

"A namespace (sometimes also called a name scope) is an abstract container or environment created to hold a logical grouping of unique identifiers or symbols (i.e., names). An identifier defined in a namespace is associated only with that namespace. The same identifier can be independently defined in multiple namespaces."

- Wikipedia

Namespaces were introduced into PHP from version 5.3 onwards. In PHP, a namespace is defined using a namespace block.

In the PHP world, namespaces are designed to solve two problems, which authors of libraries and applications encounter when creating reusable code elements, such as classes or functions:

- ◆ Ability to avoid name collisions between the code you create, and internal PHP classes/functions/constants or third-party classes/functions/constants
- ◆ Ability to alias (or shorten) extra-long names designed to alleviate the first problem, improving the readability of the source code

PHP namespaces provide a way to group related classes, interfaces, functions, and constants. Here is an example of a namespace's usage in PHP:

```
namespace My;

class Foo {
    . . .
}
namespace Your;

class Foo {
    . . .
}
```

We can use classes of the same name and reference with the PHP namespace, in the following way:

```
$myFoo = new \My\Foo();
$yourFoo = new \Your\Foo();
```

We will use My as a common root namespace for the whole application, My\Dao for our data access layer classes, and My\Service for our Service layer classes.

The API

In object-oriented languages, an API usually includes a description of a set of class definitions, with a set of behaviors associated with those classes. A behavior is a set of rules for how an object, derived from that class, will act in a given circumstance. This abstract concept is associated with the real functionalities exposed or made available by the classes, which are implemented in terms of class methods (or more generally, by all its public components, hence all public methods, but also possibly including any internal entity made public, such as fields, constants, and nested objects).

For instance, a class representing a stack can simply expose two methods publicly—push() (to add a new item to the stack), and pop() (to extract the last item, ideally placed on top of the stack).

In this case, the API can be interpreted as two methods—pop() and push(). More generally, the idea is, one can use methods of the Stack class that implements the behavior of a stack (pile exposing its top to add/remove elements).

So far, so good. We have the concepts about our project, and we know NetBeans features very well. Now, let's get down to the development...

Designing the database

In this section, we will design our MySQL database. Since we learned how to create a database connection, new database, new table, and how to run a MySQL query inside NetBeans in *Chapter 3*, *Building a Facebook-like Status Poster Using NetBeans*, we won't discuss them again, but we'll have a look at the database schema definition.

```
CREATE TABLE 'users' (
  'id' bigint(20) NOT NULL AUTO_INCREMENT,
  'useremail' varchar(50) NOT NULL,
  'password' char(32) NOT NULL,
  'userhash' char(32) NOT NULL,
  'userlevel' tinyint(4) NOT NULL,
  'username' varchar(100) NOT NULL,
  'phone' varchar(20) NULL,
  'timestamp' int(11) unsigned NOT NULL,
  PRIMARY KEY ('id'),
  UNIQUE KEY 'useremail' ('useremail')
) ENGINE=InnoDB  DEFAULT CHARSET=utf8;
```

As you can see, we have id (auto incremented with each entry) as the primary key and useremail as the unique key in the users table. We have a password field to store the user's password to up to 32 characters; userhash of 32 characters will store the user's login session identifier; userlevel to define the user's access level, for example, a normal user as 1, an admin user as 9, and so on; a username field to support maximum 100 characters; a phone field to store a user's contact number; and a timestamp field to keep track of a user's registration time. The database engine chosen is **InnoDB**, as it supports transactions and foreign keys over the **MyISAM** engine, to avoid table locking during insert and update operations by any user.

So, all you need to do is to create a new database named user, just type in the MySQL query inside the NetBeans query editor, and run the query to have your table ready in the user database.

Now, create a NetBeans PHP project and start the User API development along with the subsequent sections.

Creating the data access layer

The data access layer will consist of a User DAO class to provide database abstraction and an abstract Base DAO class to provide abstract methods, which is required for the User DAO class to be implemented. Also, we will create the abstract class to provide abstract methods for DAO classes to be created in our future projects. Note that we will use PHP namespace, My\Dao, for the data access layer classes.

Creating the BaseDao abstract class

The abstract class will be used to provide a basic framework for subclasses to implement methods. Simply, the basic database operations are CRUD or create, read, update, and delete. So, the abstract class will provide these types of abstract methods along with methods that will be required in every subclass. The BaseDao abstract class will contain the final method for database connectivity, so the subclasses don't need to write it again. To understand this better, we will keep our DAO classes in a separate directory named Dao as well.

Time for action – creating the BaseDao class

To use with a database connection, we will keep the database access credentials as their own class constants. Also, we will use PDO for all sorts of database operations. To create the Base class, go through the following steps:

1. Create a new PHP file inside the Dao directory named BaseDao.php, and type in the following class:

```php
<?php
namespace My\Dao;

abstract class BaseDao {
    private $db         = null;

    const DB_SERVER     = "localhost";
    const DB_USER       = "root";
    const DB_PASSWORD   = "root";
    const DB_NAME       = "user";


}
?>
```

You can see that this class uses `namespace My\Dao;`, and there is also an `abstract` keyword before the class name, which defines the class as abstract. This means that the class cannot be instantiated or has at least a single abstract method inside. Also, you can see the added class constants, which contain the database information and a private class variable `$db` to hold the database connection. You may modify those constants as per your requirements.

2. Now, add the following `getDb()` method in the class:

```php
protected final function getDb(){
  $dsn = 'mysql:dbname='.self::DB_NAME.';host='.self::DB_SERVER;

  try {
    $this->db = new \PDO($dsn, self::DB_USER, self::DB_PASSWORD);
  } catch (PDOException $e) {
  throw new \Exception('Connection failed: ' . $e->getMessage());
  }

  return $this->db;
}
```

The `protected final function getDb()` function connects with the MySQL database using PDO. The private variable of the class stores the PDO instance that can be used for database connectivity. Moreover, the `getDb()` method is `final` and `protected`, so the subclasses inherit this method and unable to override it.

The `$dsn` variable contains the **Data Source Name (DSN)**, which contains the information required to connect to the database. The following line creates a PDO instance to represent a connection to the requested database and returns a PDO object on its success:

```php
$this->db = new \PDO($dsn, self::DB_USER, self::DB_PASSWORD);
```

Note that the DSN throws a `PDOException` exception, if the attempt to connect to the requested database fails. We prefixed PDO with the backslash \, so PHP knows it's in the global namespace.

3. Add the following `abstract` methods to the class:

```
abstract protected function get($uniqueKey);
abstract protected function insert(array $values);
abstract protected function update($id, array $values);
abstract protected function delete($uniqueKey);
```

You can see that the methods to be implemented by the subclasses are denoted as `abstract protected`, and the `get()` method will be used to select a single entry from the table based on a unique table key, `insert()` will insert a row into the table, `update()` will be used to update a row in the table, and `delete()` will be used to delete an entry. So, all these methods have been kept abstract (without the method body), as they will be implemented by using the subclasses.

What just happened?

We have the `BaseDao` abstract class ready to be inherited by the DAO classes. The PDO instance is created and returned from the method, so all the subclasses will have the `getDb()` method, and can have this returned instance to perform some sort of database tasks using PDO. Finally, subclasses will implement the `abstract` methods as per their demand. For example, in the next tutorial, the User DAO class will implement the `get()` method to select and return a single user registration information matching the user's e-mail address from the `users` table, or the Product DAO class will implement the `get()` method to select and return single product information from the `products` table matching the product ID. Hence, the intention to practice such an abstract class is to deliver the basic framework for the Dao classes.

 One of the biggest advantages of using PDO is that if we want to migrate into other SQL solutions, all we need is to adjust the DSN parameter.

Creating the User DAO class

In this tutorial, we will create the User DAO class, which will provide all sorts of database tasks inside it. This class will keep the database hidden from the consecutive layers, that is the Service layer class. So, all the consecutive layer classes will call methods from this class and have all the necessary database work done by this class, while the data storage details are completely hidden to them. So, this class will act as an intermediary between the database and the application.

Time for action – creating the User Dao class

We will keep the relevant user constants as class constants. We will write the implementation of the methods from the `BaseDao` abstract class in this class. Simply, we will add the body of those abstract methods and our own methods required into the class. So, follow the steps listed here:

1. Create a new PHP file inside the `Dao` directory named `UserDao.php`, and type in the following code:

```php
<?php
namespace My\Dao;
class UserDao extends BaseDao {
    private $db          = null;

    public function __construct() {

        $this->db = $this->getDb();
    }

}

$userDao = new \My\Dao\UserDao;
?>
```

As you can see, the class is under the `My\Dao` namespace and extends to the `BaseDao` class, so the class will have methods inherited from the parent. The Dao class has its own private `$db`, which stores the PDO instance returned by the inherited `getDb()` method; as you can see, this `$db` variable is assigned to the class constructor.

Also, you might have noticed that the `UserDao` class has been instantiated at the bottom.

2. Type in the implementation of the `get()` method (add the method to the class), so that it looks similar to the following:

```php
public function get($useremail) {
    $statement = $this->db->prepare("SELECT * FROM users WHERE
        useremail = :useremail LIMIT 1 ");
    $statement->bindParam(':useremail', $useremail);
    $statement->execute();

    if ($statement->rowCount() > 0) {
        $row = $statement->fetch();
```

```
        return $row;
    }
}
```

You can see that the `prepare()` method prepares the SQL statement to be executed by the `PDOStatement::execute()` method. As you can see, the following statement query is used to select all the columns of a row from the `users` table, while the given e-mail address in `:useremail` (parameter bound with `bindParam()`) matches the `useremail` column.

```
SELECT * FROM users WHERE useremail = :useremail LIMIT 1;
```

Finally, if a matching row is found, fetch the array containing the user details and return.

3. Type in the implementation of the `insert()` method, so that it looks similar to the following:

```php
public function insert(array $values) {
    $sql = "INSERT INTO users ";
    $fields = array_keys($values);
    $vals = array_values($values);

    $sql .= '('.implode(',', $fields).') ';

    $arr = array();
    foreach ($fields as $f) {
        $arr[] = '?';
    }
    $sql .= 'VALUES ('.implode(',', $arr).') ';

    $statement = $this->db->prepare($sql);

    foreach ($vals as $i=>$v) {
        $statement->bindValue($i+1, $v);
    }

    return $statement->execute();
}
```

The method takes the user info passed in an array, prepares the MySQL `insert` query for the `users` table, and executes the query. Note that we have kept the field names in the `$fields` array and field values in the `$vals` array extracted from the keys and values of passed arrays respectively. We have used ? in place of all the given values for the prepared statement, which will be replaced with the corresponding value bound with the `PDOStatement::bindValue()` method. `bindValue()` binds a value to a parameter.

4. Type in the implementation of the `update()` method, so that it looks similar to the following:

```php
public function update($id, array $values) {
    $sql = "UPDATE users SET ";
    $fields = array_keys($values);
    $vals = array_values($values);

    foreach ($fields as $i=>$f) {
        $fields[$i] .= ' = ? ';
    }

    $sql .= implode(',', $fields);
    $sql .= " WHERE id = " . (int)$id ." LIMIT 1 ";

    $statement = $this->db->prepare($sql);
    foreach ($vals as $i=>$v) {
        $statement->bindValue($i+1, $v);
    }

    $statement->execute();
}
```

It prepares the MySQL UPDATE query statement in the same way as *step 3*, and executes the query to update the corresponding column values in the row with the given ID.

5. You may leave the other implementation as an empty enclosing body, as follows, or you can add your own code, as required:

```php
public function delete($uniqueKey) { }
```

As we may implement the method to delete a user in future, we have left the `delete()` method's body empty.

6. Now, we need some additional methods to be written in the class. While registering a user with any e-mail address, we can check our database to see if the e-mail address already exists in the table or not. Type in the following method:

```php
public function useremailTaken($useremail) {
    $statement = $this->db->prepare("SELECT id FROM users WHERE
        useremail = :useremail LIMIT 1 ");
    $statement->bindParam(':useremail', $useremail);
    $statement->execute();

    return ($statement->rowCount() > 0 );
}
```

The `useremailTaken()` method takes an e-mail address as the parameter to check whether that e-mail ID exists or not. It does the task by running a `SELECT` query with the given e-mail address in the `WHERE` clause. If any row is found, then it means that the e-mail address already exists, and hence the method returns `true`, or otherwise `false`. With this method, we can ensure that one e-mail address can be used only once in the system, and duplicate e-mail addresses are not allowed as this is a unique field.

7. To confirm the user's password during login, type in the following `checkPassConfirmation()` method:

```
public function checkPassConfirmation($useremail, $password) {

    $statement = $this->db->prepare("SELECT password FROM users
        WHERE useremail = :useremail LIMIT 1 ");
    $statement->bindParam(':useremail', $useremail);
    $statement->execute();

    if ($statement->rowCount() > 0) {
        $row = $statement->fetch();

        return ($password == $row['password']);
    }

    return false;

}
```

The method takes `$useremail` and `$password` as the parameter, and selects the `password` column for matching the user's e-mail. Now, if no row is found matching the criteria, then it means that the user's e-mail does not exist in the table, and `false 1` is returned; and if a matching row is found, then the array is fetched from the result to obtain the password. Finally, the fetched password from the database is compared with the given password in the second parameter. If they match, then `true` is returned. So, we can use this method to confirm the password for the given corresponding user's e-mail, while the user attempts to log in with them and can easily track the status with returned Boolean values.

8. Also, we have already added a field in the `users` table named `userhash`. The field stores a hash value (random alphanumeric string) for each login session, so we want to confirm that `userhash`, in order to verify if the user is currently logged in. Type in the following method:

```
public function checkHashConfirmation($useremail, $userhash) {

    $statement = $this->db->prepare("SELECT userhash FROM users
        WHERE useremail = :useremail LIMIT 1");
```

```
$statement->bindParam(':useremail', $useremail);
$statement->execute();

if ($statement->rowCount() > 0) {
  $row = $statement->fetch();

  return ($userhash == $row['userhash']);
}

return false;
}
```

The `checkHashConfirmation()` method is the same as the previous method in
step 7 and takes `$useremail` and `$userhash` as parameters, fetches `userhash`
for the given e-mail address, and compares itself with the given `userhash`. So, the
method that can be used to compare the `userhash` is the same for both the session
and the database. If it is the same, it means that the user is currently logged in,
because each new login updates the corresponding `userhash` in the table.

What just happened?

Calling `PDO::prepare()` and `PDOStatement::execute()` for statements, which will be
issued multiple times with different parameter values, optimizes the performance of your
application, by allowing the driver to negotiate the client and/or server-side caching of the
query plan and meta information, and helps to prevent SQL injection attacks, by eliminating
the need to manually quote the parameters.

We now have the User DAO class ready, and the DAO layer is also complete inside the `Dao`
directory in our NetBeans project. So, the User DAO class is ready to provide the required
sort of database operations. The database operations can be dealt with in a way such as
we have done, so that other subsequent classes don't need to access or rewrite database
functionalities, and hence abstraction around the database has been achieved. We can add any
sort of database-related methods in this class, to make them available for the Service classes.
Now, the instantiated object will serve as a data access object, which means this object has
access to the data in the data source, and anyone can read or write data via this object.

1. Which one is correct for the `bindValue()` and `bindParam()` methods of PDO?

    a. You can only pass variables, not values using `bindParam`, and you can pass both with `bindValue`

    b. You can only pass values using `bindParam`, and you can pass only variables with `bindValue`

    c. You can pass variables using `bindParam`, and you can pass values with `bindValue`

    d. Both are the same

Now, let's create the Service layer for our API.

Creating the Service layer

The Service layer contains classes to serve applications, or simply provides a framework for the application. The application layer will communicate with this layer to have all sorts of application services, such as user authentication, user information registration, login session validation, and form validation. For a better understanding, we will keep our service classes inside a separate directory named `Service` and use the namespace `My\Service`, for the classes of this layer.

Creating the ValidatorService class

This class will perform validation tasks, such as form validation and login information validation, and also save to deliver form error messages and field values.

Time for action – creating the ValidatorService class

We will keep some validation constants in the class itself, and the class will use `My\Service` as its namespace. Follow these steps to create the `ValidatorService` class:

1. Create a new directory named `Service` under your project directory. The Service classes will be inside this directory.

2. Create a new PHP file inside the `Service` directory named `ValidatorService.php`, and type in the following class:

```php
<?php
namespace My\Service;
use My\Dao\UserDao;
```

```
class ValidatorService {

    private $values = array();
    private $errors = array();
    public $statusMsg = null;
    public $num_errors;

    const NAME_LENGTH_MIN = 5;
    const NAME_LENGTH_MAX = 100;
    const PASS_LENGTH_MIN = 8;
    const PASS_LENGTH_MAX = 32;

    public function __construct() {

    }

    public function setUserDao(UserDao $userDao){
        $this->userDao = $userDao;
    }

}

$validator = new \My\Service\ValidatorService;
$validator->setUserDao($userDao);
?>
```

Note that the class is under the `My\Service` namespace and imports the `My\Dao\UserDao` class.

You can see the class variable `$values`, which holds the submitted form values; `$errors`, which holds the submitted form error messages; `$statusMsg`, which holds the submitted status message that is success or temporary information; and `$num_errors`, which holds the number of errors in submitted form.

We also added class constants for validation purposes. We keep the username length within 5 and 100 characters and the `password` field length between 8 and 32 characters.

As the class is dependent on the `UserDao` class, we injected the `$userDao` object inside, using a `setter` method `setUserDao()`; the `$userDao` object passed is stored in a class variable, so that the DAO can be used in other methods as well.

3. Now, fill in the class constructor, so that it looks similar to the following:

```
public function __construct() {

    if (isset($_SESSION['value_array']) && isset($_SESSION['error_
array'])) {
        $this->values = $_SESSION['value_array'];
        $this->errors = $_SESSION['error_array'];
        $this->num_errors = count($this->errors);

        unset($_SESSION['value_array']);
        unset($_SESSION['error_array']);
    } else {
        $this->num_errors = 0;
    }

    if (isset($_SESSION['statusMsg'])) {
        $this->statusMsg = $_SESSION['statusMsg'];
        unset($_SESSION['statusMsg']);
    }
}
```

You can see that both `$_SESSION['value_array']` and `$_SESSION['error_array']` have been checked initially. If they have some value set, then assign them to the corresponding class variables, as shown in the following example:

```
$this->values = $_SESSION['value_array'];
$this->errors = $_SESSION['error_array'];
$this->num_errors = count($this->errors);
```

Also, `num_errors` has been adjusted with the count of the `errors` array. Note that values in `$_SESSION['value_array']` and `$_SESSION['error_array']` will be set by the application class from where this service API will be used. These session variables have been unset immediately after grabbing their values to make them prepare for the next form submission. If these variables haven't been set, `num_errors` should be `0` (zero).

It also checks the `$_SESSION['statusMsg']` variable. If any status message has been set, grab the message into appropriate class variables and unset it.

4. Now, type in the form and error handler methods into the class, as follows:

```
public function setValue($field, $value) {
    $this->values[$field] = $value;
}

public function getValue($field) {
```

```
        if (array_key_exists($field, $this->values)) {
            return htmlspecialchars(stripslashes($this-
>values[$field]));
        } else {
            return "";
        }
    }

    private function setError($field, $errmsg) {
        $this->errors[$field] = $errmsg;
        $this->num_errors = count($this->errors);
    }

    public function getError($field) {
        if (array_key_exists($field, $this->errors)) {
            return $this->errors[$field];
        } else {
            return "";
        }
    }

    public function getErrorArray() {
        return $this->errors;
    }
```

In these class methods, you can see that setValue($field, $value) and getValue($field) methods are used to set and get the value of a single corresponding field, respectively. Similarly, setError($field, $errmsg) and getError($field) set and get the error message for a corresponding form field value while validating, while at the same time, setError increases the num_errors value. Finally, getErrorArray() returns the complete error messages array.

5. Now, type in the value validation methods of the form field as follows:

```
public function validate($field, $value) {
    $valid = false;

    if ($valid == $this->isEmpty($field, $value)) {

        $valid = true;
        if ($field == "name")
            $valid = $this->checkSize($field, $value, self::NAME_
LENGTH_MIN, self::NAME_LENGTH_MAX);

        if ($field == "password" || $field == "newpassword")
```

```
                    $valid = $this->checkSize($field, $value, self::PASS_
LENGTH_MIN, self::PASS_LENGTH_MAX);

            if ($valid)
                $valid = $this->checkFormat($field, $value);
        }

        return $valid;
    }

    private function isEmpty($field, $value) {
        $value = trim($value);
        if (empty($value)) {
            $this->setError($field, "Field value not entered");
            return true;
        }

        return false;
    }

    private function checkFormat($field, $value) {

        switch ($field) {
            case 'useremail':
                $regex = "/^[_+a-z0-9-]+(\.[_+a-z0-9-]+)*"
                       . "@[a-z0-9-]+(\.[a-z0-9-]{1,})*"
                       . "\.([a-z]{2,}){1}$/i";
                $msg = "Email address invalid";
                break;
            case 'password':
            case 'newpassword':
                $regex = "/^([0-9a-z])+$/i";
                $msg = "Password not alphanumeric";
                break;
            case 'name':
                $regex = "/^([a-z ])+$/i";
                $msg = "Name must be alphabetic";
                break;
            case 'phone':
                $regex = "/^([0-9])+$/";
                $msg = "Phone not numeric";
                break;
            default:;
```

```
    }

    if (!preg_match($regex, ( $value = trim($value)))) {
        $this->setError($field, $msg);
        return false;
    }

    return true;
}

private function checkSize($field, $value, $minLength, $maxLength)
{
    $value = trim($value);

    if (strlen($value) < $minLength || strlen($value) >
$maxLength) {
        $this->setError($field, "Value length should be within
".$minLength." & ".$maxLength." characters");
        return false;
    }

    return true;
}
```

The validation methods can be described as follows:

- `validate($field, $value)` is the entry function for validation. Methods for input validation, such as empty string checking, correct input format, or input size range, can be called from this method, and it also returns `true` if the validation passes, or `false` otherwise.

- `isEmpty($field, $value)` checks whether the string is empty or not, then sets the error message for that field and returns `false` or `true` otherwise.

- `checkFormat($field, $value)` tests fields' values against appropriate regular expressions written for each field format, sets an error (if any), and returns `false`, or otherwise `true`.

- `checkSize($field, $value, $minLength, $maxLength)` checks whether the input is within the given minimum size and maximum size.

6. We want to validate the login credentials to check whether the user e-mail exists or whether the password belongs to the user matching that user e-mail. So, add the `validateCredentials()` method as follows:

```
public function validateCredentials($useremail, $password) {

    $result = $this->userDao->checkPassConfirmation($useremail,
md5($password));

    if ($result === false) {
        $this->setError("password", "Email address or password
is incorrect");
        return false;
    }

return true;
    }
```

The method takes `$useremail` and `$password` for login credentials validation. You can see that the following line uses user Dao for confirming the password associated with the `useremail`. The Dao `checkPassConfirmation()` method returns `true` as the confirmation and `false` for either e-mail address or password is incorrect.

```
$result = $this->userDao->checkPassConfirmation($useremail,
md5($password));
```

7. When a user wants to register into our application, we can validate the e-mail address for its pre-existence. If the e-mail is not already registered in the database, then the user is free to register with that e-mail. So, type in the following method:

```
public function emailExists($useremail) {

    if ($this->userDao->useremailTaken($useremail)) {
        $this->setError('useremail', "Email already in use");
        return true;
    }

    return false;
}
```

You can see that the method uses `userDao` in `$this->userDao->useremailTaken($useremail);` to check whether the user e-mail is already taken or not. If it's taken, set the error, and return `true` as the e-mail exists.

8. Password confirmation is again required when the user wants to update the current password. So, let's add another method for validating the current password:

```
public function checkPassword($useremail, $password) {

    $result = $this->userDao->checkPassConfirmation($useremail,
md5($password));

    if ($result === false) {
    $this->setError("password", "Current password incorrect");
    return false;
}

    return true;
}
```

What just happened?

We have the validator service class ready for supporting the form, login credentials, and password validations, or even communicating with the database via userDao. Also, the validator service allows the application to retrieve temporary status messages for the guest or the user, and error messages for form input fields as well. So, it deals with all sorts of validation tasks, and the validator methods set errors if found, and return true on success or false on failure, respectively. Such error messages can be viewed, besides the corresponding form fields, as well as field values. Hence, it also helps to create the data persistence form.

Have a go hero – adding multibyte encoding support

Right now, our validator service doesn't have the ability to support multibyte character encoding. To enable the application with different character encodings such as UTF-8, you can implement the multibyte support in validation methods, such as set internal encoding, regular expression match for a multibyte string, and the use of mb_strlen() instead of strlen(). Multibyte string functions can be found at http://php.net/manual/en/ref.mbstring.php.

Creating the UserService class

The UserService class supports all the application tasks, such as login, register, or updating user details. It corresponds with the UserDao class for any sort of data-related functions and with the ValidatorService service class for any sort of validation functions. Asked by the application for tasks, such as login or register, it first calls for validation and then performs the task, while it may use DAO as required. Finally, it returns with true if the task has been accomplished, or false for any failure, such as a validation fail or any other ambiguity. Simply, applications will call the methods from the UserService class to login, register, and so on, and can know the status of the operation.

Time for action – creating the UserService class

We will use `My\Service` as the namespace for this class, and keep any constants in the class. The `UserService` class attributes will contain the user information, such as the user e-mail, user ID, username, or phone, and the constructor checks for logged in user and class variables loaded with the user details from the session. Also, the class will make use of PHP cookies to store the user's login data. The class will act as the login session manager. So initially, the class will check for the login data in sessions or in cookies that the user is logged into.

 It is recommended that you are familiar with PHP sessions and cookies for this tutorial.

So let's go through the following steps, in order to create the `UserService` class:

1. Create a new PHP file inside the `Service` directory named `UserService.php`, and type in the following class:

```php
<?php
namespace My\Service;
use My\Dao\UserDao;
use My\Service\ValidatorService;

class UserService {

    public $useremail;
    private $userid;
    public $username;
    public $userphone;
    private $userhash;
    private $userlevel;
    public $logged_in;

    const ADMIN_EMAIL = "admin@mysite.com";
    const GUEST_NAME  =  "Guest";
    const ADMIN_LEVEL = 9;
    const USER_LEVEL  =  1;
    const GUEST_LEVEL = 0;

    const COOKIE_EXPIRE =  8640000;
    const COOKIE_PATH = "/";

    public function __construct(UserDao $userDao, ValidatorService $validator) {

        $this->userDao = $userDao;
        $this->validator = $validator;
```

```
        $this->logged_in = $this->isLogin();

        if (!$this->logged_in) {
            $this->useremail = $_SESSION['useremail'] =
self::GUEST_NAME;
            $this->userlevel = self::GUEST_LEVEL;
        }
    }

}

$userService = new \My\Service\UserService($userDao, $validator);
?>
```

You can see that the class uses `namespace My\Service;`, and the Service User class may be accessed using `\My\Service\UserService`.

Check out the class variable, which stores the user data. `$logged_in` is `true` if the user is logged in.

To distinguish among users, the user-related constants have been added. Update `ADMIN_EMAIL` with your own; the administrator among the users will be defined by `ADMIN_EMAIL` and `ADMIN_LEVEL` equal to `9`. The general registered users will be defined as `USER_LEVEL` equal to `1`, and non-registered users will be defined as `GUEST_LEVEL` equal to `0` or `GUEST_NAME` as `Guest`. So, the user who registers with an e-mail address as `admin@mysite.com` will have admin access when we implement admin features.

At the cookie constant's section, `COOKIE_EXPIRE` has the cookie expiration time set to `100` days (8640000 seconds) by default, and `COOKIE_PATH` says that the cookie will be available for the whole application domain.

The cookie (a text file on the user's computer) will be used to store `useremail` as `cookname` and `userhash` as `cookid`. These cookies will be set in the case of a user-enabled option `Remember Me`. So, we will initially check to see if cookies are found on the user's local computer that match with the database, and if so, we will consider the user as a logged-in user.

Note that the constructor is injected with the `UserDao` and `ValidatorService` objects, so the class can use these dependencies inside it.

Now, with the line `$this->logged_in = $this->isLogin();` the constructor checks whether the user is logged in or not. The `private` method `isLogin()` checks for login data and if found then returns as `true`, or `false` otherwise. Actually, `isLogin()` checks the session and cookies for a user's login data, and if the data is available, it loads the class variables.

Non-logged-in users will be guest users, so `useremail` and `userlevel` are set to `Guest` and `Guest Level 0`, respectively.

```
if (!$this->logged_in) {
    $this->useremail = $_SESSION['useremail'] = self::GUEST_NAME;
    $this->userlevel = self::GUEST_LEVEL;
}
```

2. Now, let's create the `isLogin()` method, so that it looks as follows:

```
private function isLogin() {

    if (isset($_SESSION['useremail']) && isset($_
SESSION['userhash']) &&
            $_SESSION['useremail'] != self::GUEST_NAME) {

        if ($this->userDao->checkHashConfirmation($_
SESSION['useremail'], $_SESSION['userhash']) === false) {
            unset($_SESSION['useremail']);
            unset($_SESSION['userhash']);
            unset($_SESSION['userid']);
            return false;
        }

        $userinfo = $this->userDao->get($_SESSION['useremail']);
        if(!$userinfo){
            return false;
        }

        $this->useremail = $userinfo['useremail'];
        $this->userid = $userinfo['id'];
        $this->userhash = $userinfo['userhash'];
        $this->userlevel = $userinfo['userlevel'];
        $this->username = $userinfo['username'];
        $this->userphone = $userinfo['phone'];
        return true;

    }

    if (isset($_COOKIE['cookname']) && isset($_COOKIE['cookid']))
{
        $this->useremail = $_SESSION['useremail'] = $_
COOKIE['cookname'];
        $this->userhash = $_SESSION['userhash'] = $_
COOKIE['cookid'];
        return true;
```

```
    }

    return false;
}
```

If `$_SESSION` has `useremail`, `userhash`, and `useremail` not as `guest`, then it means that the user has already logged in to the data. If so, we want to confirm `userhash` and the associated `useremail` for security with the `checkHashConfirmation()` method of `UserDao`. If not confirmed, then unset the `$_SESSION` variable, and consider it as not logged in, by returning it as `false`.

Finally, if all is well, load the logged-in user's details using `Dao` at `$userinfo = $this->userDao->get($_SESSION['useremail']);;` load the class and session variables, and return it as `true`.

Again, if `$_SESSION` doesn't have the logged-in data, then we'll choose to check into cookies also, as the user may have enabled the `Remember Me` option. These cookies are set if the user is asked to remember him when he logs in. So, if the necessary data is found in cookie variables, then the class and session variables are loaded from there.

3. Now, create the login service for the applications as follows:

```
public function login($values) {

    $useremail = $values['useremail'];
    $password = $values['password'];
    $rememberme = isset($values['rememberme']);

    $this->validator->validate("useremail", $useremail);
    $this->validator->validate("password", $password);

    if ($this->validator->num_errors > 0) {
        return false;
    }

    if (!$this->validator->validateCredentials($useremail,
$password)) {
        return false;
    }


    $userinfo = $this->userDao->get($useremail);
    if(!$userinfo){
        return false;
```

```
    }

    $this->useremail = $_SESSION['useremail'] =
$userinfo['useremail'];
    $this->userid = $_SESSION['userid'] = $userinfo['id'];
    $this->userhash = $_SESSION['userhash'] = md5(microtime());
    $this->userlevel = $userinfo['userlevel'];
    $this->username = $userinfo['username'];
    $this->userphone = $userinfo['phone'];


    $this->userDao->update($this->userid, array("userhash" =>
$this->userhash));


    if ($rememberme == 'true') {
        setcookie("cookname", $this->useremail, time() +
self::COOKIE_EXPIRE, self::COOKIE_PATH);
        setcookie("cookid", $this->userhash, time() +
self::COOKIE_EXPIRE, self::COOKIE_PATH);
    }

    return true;
}
```

This method takes login details, such as `useremail`, `password`, and `rememberme`, and passes them in the `$values` array from the application. It calls for validation of the given input, returns as `false` if an error is found, and validates the association of access credentials afterwards. If all the cases have passed the validation, it will load the user information from the Dao. Note that in the following line, `md5(microtime())` creates a random string of alphanumeric characters and is assigned to the class variables.

```
$this->userhash = $_SESSION['userhash'] = md5(microtime());
```

Finally, for new login sessions to be initiated, update the corresponding user's `userhash` in the table that will be the identifier for the current session.

```
$this->userDao->update($this->userid, array("userhash" =>
    $this->userhash));
```

So, `$_SESSION` userhash and database `userhash` should be the same for an active, logged-in session.

Also, you can see, if `$rememberme` is `true`, then the cookie is set using PHP's `setcookie()` method, and the cookie is set with a name, value, and its expiration time.

4. Now, add the user registration service method as follows:

```
public function register($values) {
    $username = $values['name'];
    $useremail = $values['useremail'];
    $password = $values['password'];
    $phone = $values['phone'];

    $this->validator->validate("name", $username);
    $this->validator->validate("useremail", $useremail);
    $this->validator->validate("password", $password);
    $this->validator->validate("phone", $phone);

    if ($this->validator->num_errors > 0) {
        return false;
    }

    if($this->validator->emailExists($useremail)) {
        return false;
    }

    $ulevel = (strcasecmp($useremail, self::ADMIN_EMAIL) == 0) ?
self::ADMIN_LEVEL : self::USER_LEVEL;

    return $this->userDao->insert(array(
        'useremail' => $useremail, 'password' => md5($password),
        'userlevel' => $ulevel, 'username' => $username,
        'phone' => $phone, 'timestamp' => time()
        ));

}
```

This method takes the user details for registration, passes them in the `$values` array, and validates them. If validation gets passed, it packages the user registration details into an array, and saves them to the database using the `insert()` method of User Dao.

Note that the user level is determined by comparing a registrant's e-mail address with `ADMIN_EMAIL`.

5. Add the getUser() method as follows, to provide user information matching a given useremail parameter:

```
public function getUser($useremail){

    $this->validator->validate("useremail", $useremail);

    if ($this->validator->num_errors > 0) {
        return false;
    }
    if (!$this->validator->emailExists($useremail)) {
        return false;
    }

    $userinfo = $this->userDao->get($useremail);

    if($userinfo){
        return $userinfo;
    }

    return false;
}
```

Note that useremail is validated before delivering user information. So, the application will use this method whenever any user information is required.

6. Now, add the update() method for the user's details modification.

```
public function update($values) {
    $username = $values['name'];
    $phone = $values['phone'];
    $password = $values['password'];
    $newPassword = $values['newpassword'];

    $updates = array();

    if($username) {
        $this->validator->validate("name", $username);
        $updates['username'] = $username;
    }

    if($phone) {
        $this->validator->validate("phone", $phone);
        $updates['phone'] = $phone;
```

```
    }

    if($password && $newPassword){
        $this->validator->validate("password", $password);
        $this->validator->validate("newpassword", $newPassword);
    }

    if ($this->validator->num_errors > 0) {
        return false;
    }

    if($password && $newPassword){
        if ($this->validator->checkPassword($this->useremail,
$password)===false) {
            return false;
        }

        $updates['password'] = md5($newPassword);
    }

    $this->userDao->update($this->userid, $updates);

    return true;
}
```

Note that the method validates the given information (if any) first. If it passes the validation criteria, the corresponding column(s) value changes into the database table via User Dao.

7. The `logout()` method can be added as follows:

```
public function logout() {

        if (isset($_COOKIE['cookname']) && isset($_
COOKIE['cookid'])) {
            setcookie("cookname", "", time() - self::COOKIE_
EXPIRE, self::COOKIE_PATH);
            setcookie("cookid", "", time() - self::COOKIE_EXPIRE,
self::COOKIE_PATH);
        }

        unset($_SESSION['useremail']);
        unset($_SESSION['userhash']);

        $this->logged_in = false;
```

```
            $this->useremail = self::GUEST_NAME;
            $this->userlevel = self::GUEST_LEVEL;
    }
```

The `logout` method unsets all the cookies and session variables, sets
`$this->logged_in` to `false`, and the user becomes a guest user again.

What just happened?

We can now check if a user is logged in or not and whether the user is asked to remember
the login details, so the user doesn't want to log in with the Remember Me option again.
The class serves for login, logout, user registration, and update or retrieval of the user
information to the application layer. It uses the validator service before proceeding with the
Dao layer. So, the class ensures the data security as well, which makes the `UserService`
class ready at the service layer.

Finally, we have our API ready to work, and by using this API, we can build an application for
user registration, user profile update, login, and logout. We have our data access layer and
the service layer operational. Now, let's have a look at our NetBeans project directory.

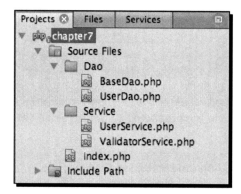

For a better understanding, we have used a separate directory and a separate namespace for
each layer. Now, we will include the API in our application file, and by using the User Service
object, we will be achieving our application's goals.

Pop quiz – using namespaces

1. Which features does the PHP namespace support?

    a. Aliasing a class name

    b. Aliasing an interface name

    c. Aliasing a namespace name

    d. Importing a function or constant

2. Which one will import a global class named `foo`?

    a. namespace foo;

    b. use foo;

    c. import foo;

    d. None of the above

Building the application

In this tutorial, we will build the application that is capable of dealing with the user registration tasks, such as registration form handling, saving user data via API, or displaying error messages, and user login and logout tasks. In our next section, we will build the PHP application, and then add the application user interfaces.

Before proceeding, keep in mind that all we have is the service layer classes. We'll choose to build the application in such a way that our application stands on top of the service layer. For this section, we don't need to think about the underlying database or Dao, rather we need to think from the application developer's perspective.

Time for action – creating the user application

We will integrate the API into our user application file, which will be the main application file; there might be interfaces or view files for each application purpose. Let's go through the following steps:

1. Create a new PHP file inside the project directory named `UserApplication.php`, and type in the following `UserApplication` class:

```php
<?php
namespace My\Application;
use My\Service\UserService;
use My\Service\ValidatorService;
session_start();

require_once    "Dao/BaseDao.php";
require_once    "Dao/UserDao.php";
require_once    "Service/ValidatorService.php";
require_once    "Service/UserService.php";


class UserApplication {
```

```php
    public function __construct (UserService $userService,
ValidatorService $validator) {

        $this->userService = $userService;
        $this->validator = $validator;

        if (isset($_POST['login'])) {

            $this->login();
        }
        else if (isset($_POST['register'])) {

            $this->register();
        }
        else if (isset($_POST['update'])) {

            $this->update();
        }
        else if ( isset($_GET['logout']) ) {

            $this->logout();

        }
    }

}

$userApp = new \My\Application\UserApplication($userService,
$validator);
?>
```

At the top of the file, you can see that after the constructor declarations, the PHP session started with `session_start()`. The API files have been included, and the class constructor has been injected with the `User` and `Validator Service` objects, so these objects become available throughout the application.

You can see that appropriate methods are called from the constructor depending on the user's request, such as `$this->login();` is called if `$_POST['login']` is set. So, all the methods are called from the constructor, and shall have the following functions:

- ❑ `login()`
- ❑ `register()`
- ❑ `update()`
- ❑ `logout()`

At the bottom of the file, we have the line `$userApp = new \My\Application\UserApplication($userService, $validator);`, which instantiates the `UserApplication` class along with the dependency injection.

2. Type in the following `login()` method:

```
public function login() {

    $success = $this->userService->login($_POST);

    if ($success) {
        $_SESSION['statusMsg'] = "Successful login!";
    } else {
        $_SESSION['value_array'] = $_POST;
        $_SESSION['error_array'] = $this->validator-
>getErrorArray();
    }

    header("Location: index.php");
}
```

You can see that the method calls the user service with the login credentials posted from the user interface in the following line:

```
$success = $this->userService->login($_POST);
```

If the login attempt is successful, it sets the success status message in the `$_SESSION['statusMsg']` session variable, and if it fails, it sets the `$_POST` array posted by the user into `$_SESSION['value_array']`, with an error array obtained from the validator object into `$_SESSION['error_array']`. Finally, it is redirected to the `index.php` page.

3. Type in the following `register()` method:

```
public function register() {

    $success = $this->userService->register($_POST);


    if ($success) {
        $_SESSION['statusMsg'] = "Registration was successful!";
        header("Location: index.php");
    } else {
        $_SESSION['value_array'] = $_POST;
        $_SESSION['error_array'] = $this->validator->getErrorArray();
        header("Location: register.php");
    }
}
```

You can see that if the registration attempt fails, it resets the corresponding session variables and is redirected to the `register.php` page, which is the user registration page.

4. Type in the following `update()` method:

```
public function update() {

    $success = $this->userService->update($_POST);


    if ($success) {
        $_SESSION['statusMsg'] = "Successfully Updated!";
        header("Location: profile.php");
    } else {
        $_SESSION['value_array'] = $_POST;
        $_SESSION['error_array'] = $this->validator->getErrorArray();
        header("Location: profileedit.php");
    }
}
```

You can see that if the user profile update attempt fails, then it resets the corresponding session variables and is redirected to the `profileedit.php` page, which is the profile edit page, or is redirected to `profile.php` on success. So, these pages will be our user profile view and update page.

5. Type in the following `logout()` method that simply calls the logout service:

```
public function logout(){

    $success = $this->userService->logout();
    header("Location: index.php");
}
```

What just happened?

Now our main application class is ready and the functionalities are as well. So we can register, log in, update, and log out a user using the application. Note that our application is just communicating via service objects, and you can feel that the application is not interested in the data sources; all it is doing is utilizing the service designed for it. In this fashion, we may write more interesting applications for the users, such as registered user list viewing; develop admin features, such as update any user or remove any user and even promote a user from normal to admin by just updating `userlevel`. It will be fun to add more features in terms of methods in different layers, to obtain a specific application.

In our next and final section, we will just add user interfaces or pages for a particular functionality.

Creating the user interface

We will create simple user interfaces and forms for user registration and login. Also, we will provide some user menus for viewing the user profile, updating the profile, and to log out. We shall integrate `UserApplication.php` at the very top of our interface files. Our interface files will consist of simple HTML with PHP code integrated inside.

Time for action – creating the user interface

We will integrate the user application file at the very beginning of each interface file. So, follow these steps to create various user interfaces:

1. Open `index.php` and integrate the `UserApplication` class so that it looks as follows:

```php
<?php
  require_once 'UserApplication.php';
?>
<!DOCTYPE html>
<html>
  <head>
    <meta http-equiv="Content-Type" content="text/html;
      charset=UTF-8">
    <title></title>
  </head>
<body>

</body>
</html>
```

And all the interface codes can be inside the body tag.

2. Now, let's create a logged-in user menu that shows the status message (if any), logged-in username, and menus at the top of each page. Create a new PHP file named `menu.php`, and type in the following code:

```php
<?php

if (isset($validator->statusMsg)) {
    echo "<span style=\"color:#207b00;\">" . $validator->statusMsg
. "</span>";
}

if ($userService->logged_in) {
    echo "<h2>Welcome $userService->username!</h2>";
```

```
          echo "<a href='profile.php'>My Profile</a> | "
          . "<a href='profileedit.php'>Edit Profile</a> | "
          . "<a href='UserApplication.php?logout=1'>Logout</a> ";
    }
?>
```

You can see that if `$validator->statusMsg` is available, then we displayed it inside the colored `span` tag. Also, if the user is logged in, then it displays the user name inside the `<h2>` tag and displays `anchor` tags for profile view, edit profile, and logging out. Now, in our pages, we will include this menu inside the `<body>` tag as follows:

```
include 'menu.php';
```

3. Now, let's create the user registration page, `register.php`, and type in the following code:

```
<?php
require_once 'UserApplication.php';
?>
<!DOCTYPE html>
<html>
    <head>
        <meta http-equiv="Content-Type" content="text/html;
charset=UTF-8">
        <title></title>
    </head>
    <body>
        <?php

        include 'menu.php';

        if (!$userService->logged_in) {
            ?>

            <h2>User Registration</h2><br />
            <?php

            if ($validator->num_errors > 0) {
                echo "<span style=\"color:#ff0000;\">" .
$validator->num_errors . " error(s) found</span>";
            }
            ?>

<form action="UserApplication.php" method="POST">
Name: <br />
```

```
<input type="text" name="name" value="<?= $validator-
>getValue("name") ?>"> <? echo "<span style=\"color:#ff0000;\">".$
validator->getError("name")."</span>"; ?>
<br />
Email: <br />
<input type="text" name="useremail" value="<?= $validator-
>getValue("useremail") ?>"> <? echo "<span style=\"color:#ff0000;\
">".$validator->getError("useremail")."</span>"; ?>
<br />
Password:<br />
<input type="password" name="password" value=""> <? echo "<span
style=\"color:#ff0000;\">".$validator->getError("password")."</
span>"; ?>
<br />
Phone: <br />
<input type="text" name="phone" value="<?= $validator-
>getValue("phone") ?>"> <? echo "<span style=\"color:#ff0000;\">".
$validator->getError("phone")."</span>"; ?>
<br /><br />
<input type="hidden" name="register" value="1">
<input type="submit" value="Register">
</form>
<br />
        Already registered? <a href="index.php">Login here</a>
    <?php
    }
    ?>
  </body>
</html>
```

You can see the user registration form displayed when the user is not logged in. `Number of errors` shows before the form with `$validator->num_errors`, if it has any errors.

In the following line, you can see that the form will be posted to the `UserApplication.php` file:

```
<form action="UserApplication.php" method="POST">
```

The form consists of four input boxes for name, e-mail, password, and phone number, and a submit button for form submission. The form comes with a hidden, input field that has a preloaded value. This hidden field value will be used to identify the login task by the `UserApplication` class constructor, in order to call the appropriate method.

4. Now, let's have a look into an input field as follows:

```
Name: <br />
<input type="text" name="name" value="<?= $validator->
  getValue("name") ?>"> <? echo "<span style=
  \"color:#ff0000;\">".$validator->getError("name")."</span>"; ?>
```

You can see that the field value has been dumped (if available using `$validator->getValue("name")`) at the `value` attribute. The field value can be found at the `validator` method using the field name during form validation. Also, by using `$validator->getError("name")`, any error associated with the `name` field will be displayed. So, the rest of the fields are designed to be alike.

5. To test form validation, point your browser with `register.php`; click on the **Register** button to submit the form without filling any field. The form looks similar to the following screenshot with an error indicated beside each field.

User Registration

4 error(s) found

Name:

[   ] Field value not entered

Email:

[   ] Field value not entered

Password:

[   ] Field value not entered

Phone:

[   ] Field value not entered

(Register)

Already registered? Login here

You can see that the form is displayed with errors for each field, and at the top of the form, the number of errors has been displayed. So, our validator and user services are working. Hence, you can test the registration form for written validation cases, and finally fill-in the form to register yourself and check the database table for your submitted information.

6. Now, let's create the login form inside the `index.php` file, at the `<body>` tag with the `Remember me` option, so that the body tag contains the following code:

```php
<?php
include 'menu.php';

if (!$userService->logged_in) {
?>

    <h2>User Login</h2>
    <br />
    <?php

    if ($validator->num_errors > 0) {
        echo "<span style=\"color:#ff0000;\">" . $validator->num_
errors . " error(s) found</span>";
    }
    ?>

<form action="UserApplication.php" method="POST">
Email: <br />
<input type="text" name="useremail" value="<?= $validator-
>getValue("useremail") ?>"> <? echo "<span style=\"color:#ff0000;\
">".$validator->getError("useremail")."</span>"; ?>
<br />
Password:<br />
<input type="password" name="password" value=""> <? echo "<span
style=\"color:#ff0000;\">".$validator->getError("password")."</
span>"; ?>
<br />
<input type="checkbox" name="rememberme" <?=($validator-
>getValue("rememberme") != "")?"checked":""?>>
<font size="2">Remember me next time </font>
<br />
<input type="hidden" name="login" value="1">
<input type="submit" value="Login">
</form>
    <br />
    New User? <a href="register.php">Register here</a>
<?php
}
?>
```

7. Check out the login form; the fields have been organized in the same way as the registration form. The form contains a hidden field name `login` and `value` set to `1`. So when the form is posted, the application class can identify that the login form has been submitted, and hence the application login method has been called. The login form page looks similar to the following:

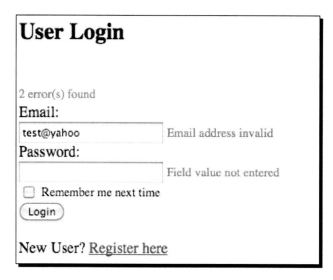

8. Test the login form with your registered data and log in. After a successful login, you will be redirected to the same page, as follows:

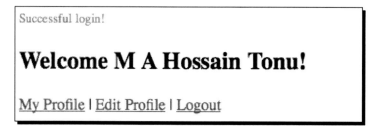

You can see the green-colored, **Successful login** status at the top of the page, and as the user is logged in, the login form is no longer required.

9. Now, create the `profile.php` profile page (you can create the file from any interface page by selecting **File | Save As…** from menu and modify it inside the body tag), as it is supposed to have the following code inside the `body` tag:

```php
<?php
include 'menu.php';

if ($userService->logged_in) {
    echo '<h2>User Profile</h2>';

    echo "Name : " . $userService->username . "<br />";
    echo "Email: " . $userService->useremail . "<br />";
    echo "Phone: " . $userService->userphone . "<br />";
}
?>
```

In this code snippet, you can see that the logged-in user's profile information is dumped, which looks similar to the following:

> # Welcome M A Hossain Tonu!
>
> My Profile | Edit Profile | Logout
>
> ## User Profile
>
> Name : M A Hossain Tonu
> Email: mahtonu@gmail.com
> Phone: 8801716668053

10. Now, create the profile edit page, `profileedit.php`, and type in the following code:

```php
<?php
include 'menu.php';

if ($userService->logged_in) {
    ?>

    <h2>Edit Profile</h2><br />

    <?php
```

```
        if ($validator->num_errors > 0) {
            echo "<span style=\"color:#ff0000;\">" . $validator->num_
errors . " error(s) found</span>";
        }
        ?>


<form action="UserApplication.php" method="POST">
Name: <br />
<input type="text" name="name" value="<?= ($validator-
>getValue("name") != "") ? $validator->getValue("name")
: $userService->username ?>"> <? echo "<span
style=\"color:#ff0000;\">" . $validator->getError("name") . "</
span>"; ?>
<br />
Password:<br />
<input type="password" name="password" value=""> <? echo "<span
style=\"color:#ff0000;\">" . $validator->getError("password") .
"</span>"; ?>
<br />
New Password: <font size="2">(Leave blank to remain password
unchanged)</font><br />
<input type="password" name="newpassword" value=""> <? echo "<span
style=\"color:#ff0000;\">" . $validator->getError("newpassword") .
"</span>"; ?>
<br />
Phone: <br />
<input type="text" name="phone" value="<?= ($validator-
>getValue("phone") != "") ? $validator->getValue("phone")
: $userService->userphone ?>"> <? echo "<span
style=\"color:#ff0000;\">" . $validator->getError("phone") . "</
span>"; ?>
<br /><br />
<input type="hidden" name="update" value="1">
<input type="submit" value="Save">
</form>
    <?php
}
?>
```

This form contains the user profile update fields, such as name, password, and phone; note that if any field such as password remains blank, then the field won't be updated. Finally, while testing, the form looks similar to the following:

Welcome M A Hossain Tonu!

My Profile | Edit Profile | Logout

Edit Profile

Name:

M A Hossain Tonu

Password:

New Password: (Leave blank to remain password unchanged)

Phone:

8801716668053

(Save)

11. Now we can test the logout feature. Check out the menu file for the logout, `anchor` tag, as follows:

```
<a href='UserApplication.php?logout=1'>Logout</a>
```

You can see that it has directly anchored the `UserApplication.php` file with a `logout=1` URL segment, so the `UserApplication` constructor finds that logout has been called with `$_GET['logout']`, and calls the application logout. Logging out redirects you to the index page.

What just happened?

We just created and tested our newly built user interfaces. The test was fun while registering the user, logging in, or updating the user profile. Keep in mind that we can use this login application in our upcoming projects, or can easily integrate new features with minimal cost. Our goal to create a layered architecture and build the application according to that design has been achieved.

The complete project source code for this chapter can be downloaded from the Packt Publishing website. Also you can fork an extended version of this project at GitHub: `https://github.com/mahtonu/login-script`.

Pop quiz – the application architecture

1. How many layers do we have in our application architecture?

   a. 2

   b. 3

   c. 4

   d. 5

2. Database abstraction is achieved in which layer?

   a. Data storage layer

   b. Data access layer

   c. Abstraction layer

   d. All of the above

3. In our application, which method directly communicates with the database for e-mail address existence?

   a. `useremailTaken()`

   b. `emailExists()`

   c. `checkEmail()`

   d. `confirmEmail()`

Have a go hero – creating admin features

As you have already noticed, we have created a database table column to define the admin user. So, implement admin features in the user service, such as a method to determine whether a user is the admin or not; if he/she is the admin, then add the admin page/interface method to get all user lists from user Dao, and display these user details, and so on. Again, you can implement the admin feature to promote a general user to the admin user, by updating the `userlevel` column.

Summary

In this chapter, we have developed the user registration, login, and logout application with a layered design. We are now confident with enterprise system architecture, and can easily add or remove features into or from the developed application.

We have specially worked on:

- Designing application architecture
- Understanding the DAO pattern
- Creating the DAO classes
- Creating the service classes
- Creating the application for user registration, login, and logout
- Developing the user interface

So, we have entered into professional PHP project development and practices of IDE features, which has helped us tremendously. We may use this project in our future web applications, where the user login facility is required; this is the advantage of "developing once, updating little, and using all the time".

Introducing Symfony2 Support in NetBeans 7.2

Symfony is a framework for PHP that allows you to develop web applications. It helps enormously in building complex web applications in PHP. While Symfony was designed to work from the command line, the NetBeans 7.2 support for Symfony lets you use it in the NetBeans graphic user interface.

This tutorial demonstrates the built-in support for the Symfony framework in NetBeans IDE 7.2 for PHP. It shows how to set up the IDE to use Symfony, how to create a PHP project that uses the Symfony framework, and a number of tips on navigating the project and setting up IDE options.

Downloading and integrating the latest Symfony Standard Edition

The Symfony Standard Edition is the best distribution to use when starting a new project. It contains the most common bundles, and comes with a simple configuration system.

Time for action – integrating Symfony2 with NetBeans

In this section, we will download the standard edition and integrate the archive to the IDE. So let's try it.

1. Download the latest Symfony Standard 2.x.x.zip from `http://symfony.com/ download`. Save the `.zip` archive to your disk; you do not need to extract the `.zip` file.

2. Check for the PHP 5 interpreter that has been added to the IDE for all the projects. Choose **Tools | Options | PHP | General**, and verify the interpreter path added in the **PHP 5 Interpreter** field. PHP interpreter is required to be added to run Symfony commands from NetBeans.

3. Now, provide the path to Symfony Standard Edition (`.zip` file) in the IDE. Choose **Tools | Options | PHP | Symfony2**. Browse the downloaded `symfony2 .zip` archive, and press **Ok** to save the settings.

What just happened?

The IDE will make use of the added `symfony2` archive each time to extract and dump a new Symfony project. The downloaded framework edition contains demo Symfony applications. We can play with those demo applications later on to have a better grasp of the Symfony framework.

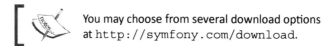 You may choose from several download options at `http://symfony.com/download`.

Creating a new Symfony2 project

As we have already integrated the Symfony2 framework installation archive with the IDE, creating a new Symfony2 project is just the same as the creation of a new PHP project in NetBeans. The IDE uses the installation archive and creates a new PHP project with the Symfony framework inside it.

Time for action – creating a Symfony2 project using NetBeans

We will create a new PHP project with the Symfony2 framework support. After the project directory structure is created by the IDE, we will configure our Symfony2 website. So let's go through the following steps:

1. Create a brand new PHP project in the usual way, and in the step where you are asked to choose **PHP Frameworks**, check the **Symfony2 PHP Web Framework** checkbox, as shown in the following screenshot:

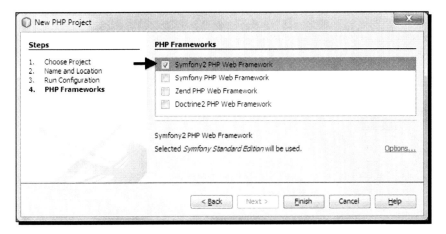

2. As soon as you click on **Finish** in the **New Project Creation** dialog box, the IDE generates a new Symfony project and dumps the extracted framework inside. The created project directory may look similar to the following:

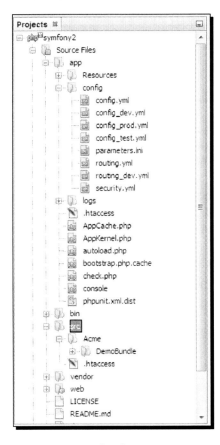

3. Now, point your browser to `http://localhost/symfony2/web/config.php` (replace `symfony2` with your project directory name). The new, Symfony2 project configuration page will look similar to the following screenshot:

Welcome!

Welcome to your new Symfony project.

This script will guide you through the basic configuration of your project. You can also do the same by editing the 'app/config/parameters.ini' file directly.

RECOMMENDATIONS

To enhance your Symfony experience, it's recommended that you fix the following :

1. Install and enable a **PHP accelerator** like APC (highly recommended).

2. Install and enable the **intl** extension.

3. Set **short_open_tag to off** in php.ini*.

* Changes to the **php.ini** file must be done in "D:\xampp\php\php.ini".

Configure your Symfony Application online ›

Bypass configuration and go to the Welcome page ›

Re-check configuration ›

You should see a welcome message from Symfony and maybe a list of problems detected by it. Try to resolve any major environment problems listed under the **Recommendations** section before continuing.

4. The Symfony framework provides a website configuration wizard. To enter the wizard, visit the **Configure your Symfony Application online** link, and configure your database credentials for the application. At this page, you may choose your database driver (`MySQL - PDO`), update your database information, such as hostname, database name, username, and password, and proceed to the next step.

   You may choose the **Bypass configuration and go to the Welcome page** link if you have already configured the application.

5. In the next step, you may generate and update a global secret code (random alphanumeric string) for your web application. This secret code is used for security purposes, such as CSRF protection.

6. The final step shows a successful configuration message, such as **Your distribution is configured!** Actually, such a configuration has overwritten the `parameters.ini` file inside the `/app/config/` directory.

7. Now, point your browser to `http://localhost/symfony2/web/app_dev.php/` (replace `symfony2` with your project directory name). The new Symfony2 project landing page will look similar to the following screenshot:

What just happened?

We have successfully created and configured a new Symfony project along with demo applications. The fundamental directory structure of a Symfony2 project is described below:

- `app/`: This includes the application configuration files, logs, caches, and so on.
- `src/`: This includes the project's PHP code and the directory your code will be in. Most likely, there will already be a demo inside it.
- `vendor/`: This includes third-party dependencies.
- `web/`: This includes the web root directory.

Getting started with Symfony at:

```
http://symfony.com/get_started
```

Understanding Symfony directory structure:

```
http://symfony.com/doc/current/quick_tour/
the_architecture.html
```

Running Symfony2 console commands inside NetBeans

NetBeans IDE supports the running of Symfony2 commands. To run the commands from the IDE, choose **Symfony2 | Run Command...** from the project's context menu to launch the **Run Symfony2 Command** dialog box. In the dialog box, you may choose your desired Symfony commands and add parameters.

For example:

```
generate:bundle [--namespace="..."] [--dir="..."] [--bundle-
name="..."] [--format="..."] [--structure]
```

The `generate:bundle` command helps you generate new bundles. By default, the command interacts with the developer to tweak the generation. Any passed option will be used as a default value for the interaction (`--namespace` is the only one needed if you follow the conventions):

```
php app/console generate:bundle --namespace=Acme/BlogBundle
```

Here, `Acme` is your identifier or company name, and `BlogBundle` is the bundle name suffixed with the string `Bundle`.

Creating a bundle

A **bundle** is similar to a plugin in other software, but even better. The key difference is that everything is a bundle in Symfony2, including both the core framework functionality and the code written for your application. Bundles are first-class citizens in Symfony2. This gives you the flexibility to use pre-built features packaged in third-party bundles or to distribute your own bundles. It makes it easy to pick and choose which features to enable in your application and to optimize them the way you want.

A bundle is simply a structured set of files within a directory that implements a single feature. You might create a **BlogBundle**, a **ForumBundle**, or a bundle for user management (many of these already exist as open source bundles). Each directory contains everything related to that feature, including PHP files, templates, stylesheets, JavaScript, tests, and so on. Every aspect of a feature exists in a bundle, and every feature lives in a bundle.

Time for action – creating a bundle using the Symfony2 console command

We are going to create a new bundle with the `generate:bundle` command using the IDE's **Run Symfony2 Command** dialog box. So let's try that...

1. In the **Projects** pane, right-click on the **Projects** node, and from the context menu choose **Symfony2 | Run Command...** to launch the **Run Symfony2 Command** dialog box, as follows:

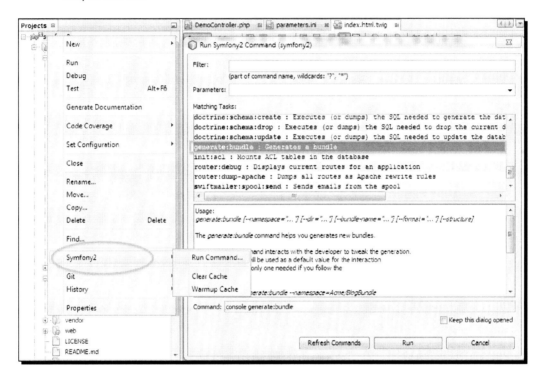

You will be able to see a list of the available commands in the **Matching Tasks** box. You can add parameters for those commands and see the complete command in the **Command** dialog box.

2. From the preceding dialog box, select the `generate:bundle` command and click on **Run**, or double-click on the listed name to run the command. The IDE's graphical console opens for prompting the namespace.

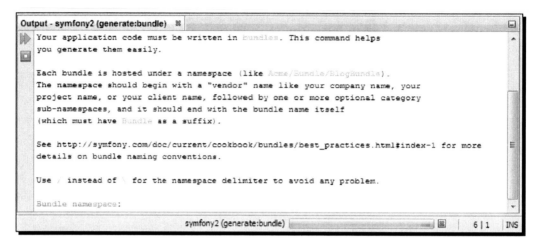

3. Enter the value for **Bundle namespace**, say `Application/FooBundle`.

4. Enter the value for **Bundle name** or press *Enter* to accept the default bundle name as `ApplicationFooBundle`.

5. Press *Enter* at the `Target` directory to accept the default bundle path as `/src`.

6. You may enter the value for **Configuration format** (`yml`, `xml`, `php`, or `annotation`) as `yml`; the default value is `annotation`.

7. Enter **Yes** for **Do you want to generate the whole directory structure [no]?** to generate a whole directory structure for the bundle; the default is no.

8. Confirm the bundle generation by entering **Yes** again.

9. At **Confirm automatic update of your Kernel [yes]?** and **Confirm automatic update of the Routing [yes]?**, press *Enter* to accept the default value, which is yes. So the bundle can be registered in the Symfony kernel and the bundle routing file is linked to the default routing configuration file.

10. Now, as you can see, a new bundle has been created inside the `/src` directory; the `bundle` directory structure looks similar to the following:

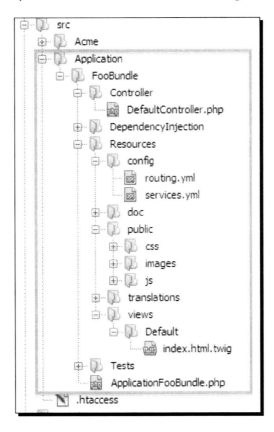

Note that the default controller, route file, template, and so on have been created simultaneously with the bundle creation.

11. Now, to test your bundle, point your browser to `http://localhost/symfony2/web/app_dev.php/hello/tonu`, and you may see an output similar to **Hello Tonu!**

12. Check out the bundle routing file at `/src/Application/FooBundle/Resources/config/routing.yml`, and you will see the URL with the pattern `/hello/{name}` mapped with the default controller's index action (`ApplicationFooBundle:Default:index`). In this example, the action displays the name passed as the URL parameter in place of `{name}`.

What just happened?

Each bundle is hosted under a namespace (such as `Acme/Bundle/BlogBundle` or `Acme/BlogBundle`). The namespace should begin with a "vendor" name, such as your company name, your project name, or your client name, followed by one or more optional category subnamespaces, and it should end with the bundle name itself (which must have `Bundle` as a suffix).

See `http://symfony.com/doc/current/cookbook/bundles/best_practices.html#index-1` for more details on bundle naming conventions.

We have seen the interactive console that asks for arguments and creates the entire `bundle` directory structure automatically. Also, it registers the bundle into Symfony's `/app/AppKernel.php`, and links the bundle routing configuration file into `default/app/config/routing.yml`.

Symfony learning resource:

`http://symfony.com/doc/current/book/index.html`

B
NetBeans Keyboard Shortcuts

The common keyboard shortcuts for the NetBeans IDE are as follows.

File menu

Keys	Command	Action
Ctrl + Shift + N	**New**	Creates a new project with the **New Project** wizard
Ctrl + N	**New**	Creates a new file with the **New File** wizard
Ctrl + Shift + O	**Open File**	Opens an existing project
Ctrl + S	**Save**	Saves the current file
Ctrl + Shift + S	**Save All**	Saves all files

Edit menu

Keys	Command	Action
Ctrl + Z	**Undo**	Reverses (one at a time) a series of editor actions, except **Save**
Ctrl + Y	**Redo**	Reverses (one at a time) a series of **Undo** commands
Ctrl + X	**Cut**	Deletes the current selection and places it on the clipboard
Ctrl + C	**Copy**	Copies the current selection to the clipboard
Ctrl + V	**Paste**	Pastes the contents of the clipboard into the insertion point

Keys	Command	Action
Ctrl + Shift + V	**Paste Formatted**	Pastes the formatted contents of the clipboard into the insertion point
Delete	**Delete**	Deletes the current selection
Ctrl + A	**Select All**	Selects everything in the current document or window
Alt + Shift + J	**Select Identifier**	Selects the current identifier
Ctrl + F3	**Find Selection**	Finds instances of the current selection
F3	**Find Next**	Finds next instance of found text
Shift + F3	**Find Previous**	Finds previous instance of found text
Ctrl + F	**Find**	Finds a text string
Ctrl + H	**Replace**	Finds a string of text and replaces it with the string specified
Alt + F7	**Find Usages**	Finds usages and subtypes of selected code
Ctrl + Shift + F	**Find in Projects**	Finds a specified text, object names, and object types within projects
Ctrl + Shift + H	**Replace in Projects**	Replaces text, object names, and object types within projects

View menu

Keys	Command	Action
Ctrl + - (minus)	**Collapse Fold**	If the insertion point is in a foldable section of text, collapses those lines into one line
Ctrl + + (plus)	**Expand Fold**	If the currently selected line in the **Source Editor** window represents several folded lines, expands the fold to show all of the lines
Ctrl + Shift + - (minus)	**Collapse All**	Collapses all foldable sections of text in the **Source Editor** window
Ctrl + Shift + + (plus)	**Expand All**	Expands all foldable sections of text in the **Source Editor** window
Alt + Shift + Enter	**Full Screen**	Expands window to full length and breadth of screen

Navigate menu

Keys	Command	Action
Alt + Shift + O	Go to File	Finds and opens a specific file
Ctrl + O	Go to Type	Finds and opens a specific class or interface
Ctrl + Alt + Shift + O	Go to Symbol	Finds and opens a specific symbol
Ctrl + Shift + T	Go to Test	Finds and opens a specific test
Ctrl + back quote	Go to Previous Document	Opens the document last opened before the current one
Ctrl + Shift + B	Go to Source	Displays the source file containing the definition of the selected class
Ctrl + B	Go to Declaration	Jumps to the declaration of the item under the cursor
Ctrl + Shift + P	Go to Super Implementation	Jumps to the super implementation of the item under the cursor
Ctrl + Q	Last Edit Location	Scrolls the editor to the last place where editing occurred
Alt + Left arrow key	Back	Navigates back
Alt + Right arrow key	Forward	Navigates forward
Ctrl + G	Go to Line	Jumps to the specified line
Ctrl + Shift + M	Toggle Bookmark	Sets a bookmark on a line of code
Ctrl + Shift + . (period)	Next Bookmark	Cycles forward through the bookmarks
Ctrl + Shift + , (comma)	Previous Bookmark	Cycles backwards through the bookmarks
Ctrl + . (period)	Next Error	Scrolls the **Source Editor** window to the line that contains the next build error
Ctrl + , (comma)	Previous Error	Scrolls the **Source Editor** window to the line that contains the previous build error
Ctrl + Shift + 1	Select in Projects	Opens the **Projects** window and selects the current document within it
Ctrl + Shift + 2	Select in Files	Opens the **Files** window and selects the current document within it
Ctrl + Shift + 3	Select in Favorites	Opens the **Favorites** window and selects the current document within it

Source menu

Keys	Command	Action
Alt + Shift + F	**Format**	Formats the selected code or the entire file if nothing is selected
Alt + Shift + Left arrow key	**Shift Left**	Moves the selected line or lines one tab to the left
Alt + Shift + Right arrow key	**Shift Right**	Moves the selected line or lines one tab to the right
Alt + Shift + Up arrow key	**Move Up**	Moves the selected line or lines one line up
Alt + Shift + Down arrow key	**Move Down**	Moves the selected line or lines one line down
Ctrl + Shift + Up arrow key	**Duplicate Up**	Copies the selected line or lines one line up
Ctrl + Shift + Down arrow key	**Duplicate Down**	Copies the selected line or lines one line down
Ctrl + / (slash) or *Ctrl + Shift + C*	**Toggle Comment**	Toggles the commenting out of the current line or selected lines
Ctrl + Space bar	**Complete Code**	Shows the code completion box
Alt + Insert	**Insert Code**	Pops up a context aware menu that you can use to generate common structures such as constructors, getters, and setters
Alt + Enter	**Fix Code**	Displays the editor hints, and the IDE informs you when a hint is available when the light bulb is displayed
Ctrl + Shift + I	**Fix Imports**	Generates the import statements required by the classes specified in the file
Ctrl + P	**Show Method Parameters**	Selects the next parameter; you must have a parameter selected (highlighted) for this shortcut to work
Ctrl + Shift + Space	**Show Documentation**	Shows the documentation for the item under the cursor
Ctrl + Shift + K	**Insert Next Matching Word**	Generates the next word used elsewhere in your code as you type its beginning characters
Ctrl + K	**Insert Previous Matching Word**	Generates the previous word used elsewhere in your code as you type its beginning characters

Refactor menu

Keys	Command	Action
Ctrl + R	**Rename**	Inplace rename
Ctrl + M	**Move**	Inplace move
Alt + Delete	**Safely Delete**	Before deleting, display references

Run menu

Keys	Command	Action
F6	**Run Main Project**	Runs the main project
Alt + F6	**Test Project**	Starts PHPUnittest for project
Shift + F6	**Run File**	Runs the currently selected file
Ctrl + F6	**Test File**	Starts PHPUnittest for current file
F11	**Build Main Project**	Compiles the file; if you select a folder, the IDE compiles all files regardless of whether they have changed since the last compile
Shift + F11	**Clean and Build Main Project**	Compiles the file; if you select a folder, the IDE compiles all files regardless of whether they have changed since the last compile
F9	**Compile File**	Compiles the file; if you select a folder, the IDE compiles only the files that are new or have changed since the last compile

Debug menu

Keys	Command	Action
Ctrl + F5	**Debug Main Project**	Debugs the main project
Ctrl + Shift + F5	**Debug File**	Starts debugging session for currently selected file
Ctrl + Shift + F6	**Debug Test for File**	Starts debugging test for file in PHPUnit
Shift + F5	**Finish Debugger Session**	Ends the debugging session

Keys	Command	Action
F5	**Continue**	Resumes debugging until the next breakpoint or the end of the program is reached
F8	**Step Over**	Executes one source line of a program. If the line is a method call, executes the entire method then stops
Shift + F8	**Step Over Expression**	Steps over the expression and then stops the debugging
F7	**Step Into**	Executes one source line of a program; if the line is a method call, executes the program up to the method's first statement and stops
Ctrl + F7	**Step Out**	Executes one source line of a program; if the line is a method call, executes the methods and returns control to the caller
F4	**Run to Cursor**	Runs the current project to the cursor's location in the file and stop program execution
Shift + F7	**Run into Method**	Runs the current project to the specified method and then steps into the method
Ctrl + Alt + Up arrow key	**Make Callee Current**	Makes the method being called the current call; only available when a call is selected in the **Call Stack** window
Ctrl + Alt + Down arrow key	**Make Caller Current**	Makes the calling method the current call; only available when a call is selected in the **Call Stack** window
Ctrl + F8	**Toggle Line Breakpoint**	Adds a line breakpoint or removes the breakpoint at the cursor location in the program
Ctrl + Shift + F8	**New Breakpoint**	Sets a new breakpoint at the specified line, exception, or method
Ctrl + Shift + F7	**New Watch**	Adds the specified variable to watch
Ctrl + F9	**Evaluate Expression**	Opens the **Evaluate Expression** dialog box

Window menu

Keys	Command	Action
Ctrl + 0	**Source Editor**	Switches to the **Source Editor** window
Ctrl + 1	**Projects**	Opens the **Projects** window
Ctrl + 2	**Files**	Opens the **Files** window
Ctrl + 3	**Favorites**	Opens the **Favorites** window
Ctrl + 4	**Output Window**	Opens the **Output** window
Ctrl + 5	**Services**	Opens the **Services** window

Keys	Command	Action
Ctrl + Shift + 5	**HTTP Monitor**	Opens the **HTTP Monitor** window
Ctrl + 6	**Task List**	Opens the **Task List** window
Ctrl + 7	**Navigator**	Opens the **Navigator**
Alt + Shift + 1	**Debugging |** Variables	Opens the **Variables Debugger** window
Alt + Shift + 2	**Debugging |** **Watches**	Opens the **Watches Debugger** window
Alt + Shift + 3	**Debugging | Call Stack**	Opens the **Call Stack Debugger** window
Alt + Shift + 4	**Debugging |** **Classes**	Opens the **Classes Debugger** window
Alt + Shift + 5	**Debugging |** **Breakpoints**	Opens the **Breakpoints Debugger** window
Alt + Shift + 6	**Debugging |** **Sessions**	Opens the **Sessions Debugger** window
Alt + Shift + 7	**Debugging |** **Threads**	Opens the **Threads Debugger** window
Alt + Shift + 8	**Debugging |** **Sources**	Opens the **Sources** window
Ctrl + W	**Close**	Closes the current tab in the current window; if the window has no tabs, the whole window is closed
Shift + Esc	**Maximize Window**	Maximizes the **Source Editor** window or the present window
Alt + Shift + D	**Undock Window**	Detaches the window from the IDE
Ctrl + Shift + W	**Close All Documents**	Closes all open documents in the **Source Editor** window
Shift + F4	**Documents**	Opens the **Documents** dialog box, in which you can save and close groups of open documents
Ctrl + Tab (Ctrl + ')	**Switch to Recent Window**	Toggles through the open windows in the order that they were last used; the dialog box displays all open windows and each of the open documents in the **Source Editor** window

Scrolling and selecting

Keys	Action
Ctrl + Down arrow key	Scrolls the window up without moving the insertion point
Ctrl + Up arrow key	Scrolls the window down without moving the insertion point
Ctrl + [	Moves the insertion point to the highlighted matching bracket; this shortcut only works when the insertion point is immediately after the opening or closing bracket
Ctrl + *Shift* + [	Selects the block between a pair of brackets; this shortcut only works when the insertion point is immediately after either the opening or closing bracket
Ctrl + *G*	Jumps to any specified line
Ctrl + *A*	Selects all text in the file

Modifying text

Keys	Action
Insert	Switches between insert text and overwrite text mode
Ctrl + *Shift* + *J*	Opens the Internationalize dialog box that you can use to insert an internationalized string at the insertion point
Ctrl + *U, U*	Makes the selected characters or the character to the right of the insertion point uppercase
Ctrl + *U, L*	Makes the selected characters or the character to the right of the insertion point lowercase
Ctrl + *U, S*	Reverses the case of the selected characters or the character to the right of the insertion point

Code folding

Keys	Action
Ctrl + - (minus)	Collapses the block of code the insertion point is on
Ctrl + + (plus)	Expands the block of code the insertion point is next to
Ctrl + *Shift* + - (minus)	Collapses all blocks of code
Ctrl + *Shift* + + (plus)	Expands all blocks of code

Searching for text

Keys	Action
Ctrl + F3	Searches for the word the insertion point is on and highlights all occurrences of that word
F3	Selects the next occurrence of the word in your current search
Shift + F3	Selects the previous occurrence of the word in your current search
Alt + Shift + H	Switches highlighting of search results on or off
Ctrl + F	Opens the **Find** dialog box
Ctrl + H	Opens the **Find and Replace** dialog box

Setting tabs

Keys	Action
Tab	Shifts all text to the right of insertion point to the right
Alt + Shift + Right	Shifts text in line containing the insertion point to the right
Alt + Shift + Left	Shifts text in line containing the insertion point to the left

The IDE also provides different profiles of preconfigured shortcuts for users who are used to the keyboard shortcuts of other editors and IDEs. You can copy and modify any keyboard shortcut profile. The IDE provides the following shortcut profiles:

◆ Eclipse

◆ Emacs

◆ IDEA

◆ NetBeans

◆ NetBeans 5.5

Since the shortcut mappings changed significantly between NetBeans IDE 5.5 and NetBeans IDE 6.0, you have the option of switching back to the shortcuts that were available in NetBeans IDE 5.5. To do so, choose the NetBeans 5.5 shortcut profile from **Tools | Options | Keymap**.

 For Mac OS keyboard shortcuts, see **NetBeans Help | IDE Basics | Keyboard Shortcuts | Mac OS Keyboard Shortcuts**.

C
Pop Quiz Answers

The answers to the pop quizzes from each chapter are provided here for your reference. How did you score?

Chapter 2, Boosting your Coding Productivity with the PHP Editor

Pop quiz – familiarizing with basic IDE features

1	d
2	d
3	c
4	c
5	b

Pop quiz – exploring the editor for PHP

1	d
2	d
3	b
4	d

Pop quiz – using rename refactoring and instant rename

1	a
2	b

Pop quiz – using code completion

1	c
2	d
3	b

Pop quiz – using code generators

1	a
2	d

Chapter 3, Building a Facebook-like Status Poster using NetBeans

Pop quiz – Understanding PDO

1	c

Pop quiz – Understanding CSS

1	b
2	a
3	b

Pop quiz – Reviewing jQuery knowledge

1	c
2	d
3	c
4	c
5	b
6	d

Chapter 4, Debugging and Testing using NetBeans

Pop quiz – debugging with XDebug

1	a, c, d
2	b
3	b

Pop quiz – PEAR

1	b

Pop quiz – unit testing and code coverage

1	d
2	c
3	c
4	c

Chapter 5, Using Code Documentation

Pop quiz – reviewing tags

1	c
2	b
3	a

Chapter 6, Understanding Git, the NetBeans way

Pop quiz – understanding Git

1	a
2	b
3	b
4	b

Pop quiz – working with Git

1	a
2	b
3	b
4	d

Pop quiz – working with remote repositories and branches

1	b
2	b
3	d

Chapter 7, Building User Registration, Login, and Logout

Pop quiz – reviewing PDO

1	c

Pop quiz – using namespaces

1	a, b, c
2	b

Pop quiz – the application architecture

1	c
2	b
3	a

Index

Thank you for buying
PHP Application Development with NetBeans Beginner's Guide

About Packt Publishing

Packt, pronounced 'packed', published its first book "*Mastering phpMyAdmin for Effective MySQL Management*" in April 2004 and subsequently continued to specialize in publishing highly focused books on specific technologies and solutions.

Our books and publications share the experiences of your fellow IT professionals in adapting and customizing today's systems, applications, and frameworks. Our solution based books give you the knowledge and power to customize the software and technologies you're using to get the job done. Packt books are more specific and less general than the IT books you have seen in the past. Our unique business model allows us to bring you more focused information, giving you more of what you need to know, and less of what you don't.

Packt is a modern, yet unique publishing company, which focuses on producing quality, cutting-edge books for communities of developers, administrators, and newbies alike. For more information, please visit our website: www.packtpub.com.

About Packt Open Source

In 2010, Packt launched two new brands, Packt Open Source and Packt Enterprise, in order to continue its focus on specialization. This book is part of the Packt Open Source brand, home to books published on software built around Open Source licences, and offering information to anybody from advanced developers to budding web designers. The Open Source brand also runs Packt's Open Source Royalty Scheme, by which Packt gives a royalty to each Open Source project about whose software a book is sold.

Writing for Packt

We welcome all inquiries from people who are interested in authoring. Book proposals should be sent to author@packtpub.com. If your book idea is still at an early stage and you would like to discuss it first before writing a formal book proposal, contact us; one of our commissioning editors will get in touch with you.

We're not just looking for published authors; if you have strong technical skills but no writing experience, our experienced editors can help you develop a writing career, or simply get some additional reward for your expertise.

PHP 5 Social Networking

ISBN: 978-1-849512-38-1   Paperback: 456 pages

Create a powerful and dynamic social networking website in PHP by building a flexible framework

1. Build a flexible Social Networking framework using PHP which can be extended to fit the needs of any Social Networking site

2. Develop a suitable structure for our framework, with MVC to structure the architecture and a Registry to store core Objects

3. Allow users to connect and communicate with each other using communication with friends list, flexible user profiles, messages, discussions, and much more

NetBeans IDE 7 Cookbook

ISBN: 978-1-849512-50-3   Paperback: 308 pages

Over 70 highly focused practical recipes to maximize your output with NetBeans

1. Covers the full spectrum of features offered by the NetBeans IDE

2. Discover ready-to-implement solutions for developing desktop and web applications

3. Learn how to deploy, debug, and test your software using NetBeans IDE

4. Another title in Packt's Cookbook series giving clear, real-world solutions to common practical problems

Please check **www.PacktPub.com** for information on our titles

CakePHP Application Development

ISBN: 978-1-847193-89-6   Paperback: 332 pages

Step-by-step introduction to rapid web development using the open-source MVC CakePHP framework

1. Develop cutting-edge Web 2.0 applications, and write PHP code in a faster, more productive way

2. Walk through the creation of a complete CakePHP Web application

3. Customize the look and feel of applications using CakePHP layouts and views

4. Make interactive applications using CakePHP, JavaScript, and AJAX helpers

jQuery 1.3 with PHP

ISBN: 978-1-847196-98-9   Paperback: 248 pages

Enhance your PHP applications by increasing their responsiveness through jQuery and its plugins.

1. Combine client-side jQuery with your server-side PHP to make your applications more efficient and exciting for the client

2. Learn about some of the most popular jQuery plugins and methods

3. Create powerful and responsive user interfaces for your PHP applications

4. Complete examples of PHP and jQuery with clear explanations

Please check **www.PacktPub.com** for information on our titles

CPSIA information can be obtained at www.ICGtesting.com
Printed in the USA
LVOW111918290812

296546LV00010B/63/P